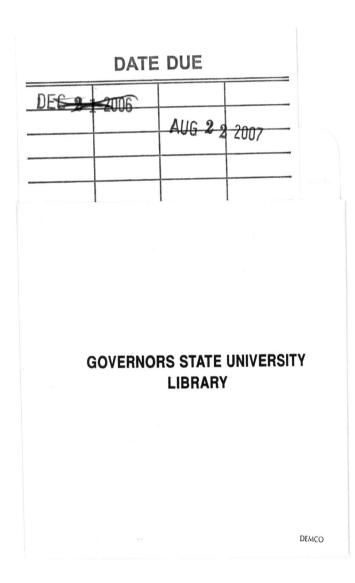

Reaching and Teaching

Stressed and

Anxious

Learners

in Grades 4-8

REACHING AND TEACHING
STRESSED AND
ANXIOUS
LEARNERS
IN GRADES 4-8

Strategies for
Relieving Distress and Trauma
in Schools and Classrooms

BARBARA E. OEHLBERG

CORWIN PRESS
A SAGE Publications Company
Thousand Oaks, California

Copyright © 2006 by Barbara E. Oehlberg

For information:

Corwin Press
A SAGE Publications Company
2455 Teller Road
Thousand Oaks, California 91320
www.corwinpress.com

Sage Publications Ltd.
1 Oliver's Yard
55 City Road
London EC1Y 1SP
United Kingdom

Sage Publications India Pvt. Ltd.
B-42, Panchsheel Enclave
Post Box 4109
New Delhi 110 017 India

Printed in the United States of America

Library of Congress Cataloging-in-Publication Data

Oehlberg, Barbara, 1932-
Reaching and teaching stressed and anxious learners in grades 4-8 : strategies
for relieving distress and trauma in schools and classrooms / Barbara E. Oehlberg.
    p. cm.
Includes bibliographical references and index.
ISBN 1-4129-1723-9 (cloth) — ISBN 1-4129-1724-7 (pbk.)
   1. Mentally ill children—Education (Elementary) 2. Mentally ill
children—Education (Middle school) 3. Stress in children—Treatment.
4. Anxiety in children—Treatment. I. Title.
LC4165.O34 2006
371.94—dc222

                                                        2005019987

This book is printed on acid-free paper.

05   06   07   08   09   10   9   8   7   6   5   4   3   2   1

Acquiring Editor:	Faye Zucker
Editorial Assistant:	Gem Rabanera
Production Editor:	Jenn Reese
Copy Editor:	Bonnie Freeman
Typesetter:	C&M Digitals (P) Ltd.
Proofreader:	Scott Oney
Indexer:	Karen McKenzie
Cover Designer:	Scott Van Atta

Contents

Foreword   ix
    Susan G. Clark

Preface   xiii

Publisher's Acknowledgments   xvi

About the Author   xvii

Introduction: Children Haven't Changed; Childhood Has   1

Glossary: The Vocabulary of Anxiety, Stress, and Trauma   5

**Part I: Brain Changes and How They Affect Student
Behaviors and Learning**   9

1. The Impact of Losses and Stress on the Student's Mind and Body   11
    Losses   11
    Stress   13
    When Traumatic Memories Are Triggered   13
    Cognitive Lockout   14
    Interventions Are Possible   16

2. Regaining Cognitive Access: The Process of Transforming
Stress and the Sense of Helplessness   17
    Transforming Perceptions of Helplessness   17
    Strengthening Self-Regulation   19

**Part II: Activities for Transforming the Helplessness
Generated by Stress and Fear**   23

3. Language Arts: Creative Writing and Journaling   25
    Topics for Creative Writing and Journaling   26
        Issues of Loss and Being Lost or Invisible   26
        Issues of Rejection or Being Excluded   27
        Issues of Brokenness, Helplessness, or Futurelessness   27
        Issues of Betrayal or Broken Promises   28
        Issues of Emotional Intelligence (Dealing With Feelings)   28
        Issues of Hope, Empowerment, and Healing   29
        Debating Points and Issues   30
        Prose and Poetry   30

Integrating Art and Creative Writing Into Core
    Curriculum Areas: Combining Art and Literary
    Themes That Can Be Applied to Core Curriculum Subjects   31
        Ad Campaigns   32
        Comic Books   32
    Mandalas   33

4. **Social Studies and History: Creative Topics**   **35**
    Historical Cartoons and Storyboards   36
    Fictional Comic Books About Historical Characters   37
    Artistic Media Projects for History or Social Studies   38
        Creating Scripts for Hypothetical Radio Interviews   38
        Writing Radio Scripts for "What if . . ." Programs   40
        Creating Public Service Announcements   40

5. **Character Education**   **43**
    Internal Strengths: Emotional Intelligence   44
        A Classroom Directory of Feelings and Emotions   45
        A Feelings Mural: Addressing All Feelings   45
        A Box of Respect: Addressing Self-Acceptance, Self-Respect,
            and the Ability to Respect and Empathize With Others   47
        The Iceberg Project: Addressing Issues of Respect,
            Empathy, and Trust   47
        Letters to Hurts: Addressing Empathy, Compassion,
            Courage, Anger Issues, Foreiveness, and Generosity   48
        Drawing a Dream: Addressing Issues of Anger, Work Ethic,
            Forgiveness, and Hopelessness   48
        Facing Fears: Addressing Fears, Courage,
            Anger, and the Ability to Overcome   49
        Playground Charters: Addressing Issues of Leadership,
            Integrity, Conflict, Hopefulness, and Justice   49
    Where Are the Heroes?   50
        Issues of Emotional Honesty, Leadership,
            Risky Behaviors, and Choices   50
        Honoring Strengths With a Character Wall   50
        The Character Board Game   51
    Physical Strengths   52
        Internal Capacities for Self-Regulation
            and Stress Management   52
        Leading a Relaxation Exercise   53

6. **Building Resiliency Through Afterschool,**
    Summer Camp, and Recreational Programming   **55**
    Afterschool Programs   55
    Specific Activities for Afterschool Programs   56
        Logos   56
        Collaborations for Creative Projects With
            Younger Children: Plays, Puppets, and Masks   57
        Designing Board Games   59
        Physical and Mental Exercises   60

Sand Trays   63
Clubs for a Sense of Belonging and Identity   64
Crossword Puzzles   67
Theater and Arts Groups or Camps   67
Drama Scripts for Stage or Radio:
    Building a World Fit for Children   67
Comedy Scripts   68
Movement and Dance   68
The Power of the Beat: The Rhythm of Healing   69
Media Production   71
Summer Camps or Activity Programs   71
Boys and Girls Clubs, Scouting, and 4-H   73

Part III: Schools That Work: A Sense of Safety for All   **75**

7. **Sustaining Enhanced Learning Environments**   **77**
Opportunities for Classroom Change   78
Avoiding the Stress of Threats   78
Alternative Responses   78
Classroom Guidelines   79
Restorative Discipline   80
"Discipline That Restores"   80
Stress Reduction Strategies for the Classroom   81

8. **School Safety Issues: Violence Prevention**   **85**
Generating a United Effort: Leadership
    and Staff Development   85
Specific Strategies for Overall Security and
    Sense of Safety Throughout the School Building   88
Strategies Specifically for Middle Schools   89
Supports for Reentering Students   89
Supports for New or Transferring Students   90
Suspension and Expulsion Policies   91
Crisis Preparation   92
Conflict and Anger Management   93
Violence Prevention Strategies   94
Early Prevention   94
Bullying   95
Inclusion   99
Restorative Justice   100

9. **Meaningful Change in the U.S. Education System**   **103**
Initiating Change From the Ground Up   104
Generating Support   104

Resource A: Crossword Puzzles   **107**

Resource B: Answers to the Crossword Puzzles   **141**

References   **159**

Index   **161**

Foreword

What lies behind us and what lies before us are tiny matters compared to what lies within us.

—Ralph Waldo Emerson

Schooling is influenced strongly by public opinion and political demands. Consequently, the aims of education are many: to transmit history, culture, and social values and to prepare students for economic productivity; for participation in a representative democracy; and for self-development and intellectual, social, and emotional growth. Behind social change is a federal or state legislative response defining expectations of schooling as equal educational opportunity and today as increased academic performance outcomes; no child is to be left behind.

There is broad consensus that a public education is the gateway to a better future and is created through economic, social, and political pressure. However, dwindling financial resources, rising tax burdens, increasing costs, outdated facilities, limited time, and public discourse directing schools to prove that students are learning more and at higher levels of achievement each year are just a few considerations. The challenge faced by educators in this climate is how to reach and teach the students before them.

As the demands for accountability in education increase, teachers are working diligently to understand the children in their classrooms. The great wonder of the public school experiment is that children join together to learn from all types of families; socioeconomic classes; and racial, cultural, and ethnic groups. School boards and universities have invested much in understanding the problems associated with teaching students who come to school with a range of differences between them and among them. Consequently, more teachers possess a class consciousness and see themselves as providers of transformative schooling, empowering students with the skills and knowledge with which they can grow into critical and questioning thinkers.

Yet in order to learn, students must be ready to learn, and so schools have responded to the needs of their students by attempting to compensate for whatever may be lacking. Parenting courses are offered, clothes are readily available to students who aren't properly dressed, breakfast programs are offered to those who are hungry. Interagency collaborations provide students and families with needed welfare, medical, and mental health services. Conflict management interventions, Alcoholics Anonymous meetings, and support groups of all kinds are available as well. Peer tutoring, afterschool workshops on test-taking strategies, and supplemental services are directed toward raising test scores. All of these services are provided to keep students in school, ensure that they are healthy, and improve their academic achievement.

One issue overlooked by many educators is that lack of student readiness and inability to learn at the pace demanded by accountability measures are not confined to marginalized, impoverished, or excluded students. Indeed, many educators make classroom decisions based on their knowledge of community and social problems. They see children's behavioral or academic changes that result from parent unemployment, homelessness, alienation, alcoholism, and drug use.

While educators acknowledge the many social problems that interfere with learning, the provision of programs designed to redirect the student toward learning and the future benefits of an education may not address the more fundamental reason that a student may not be achieving as expected: a lack of personal safety. In children who experience divorce, death, or trauma by violence or by accident, learning can be stalled or diverted to inappropriate conduct. These events, and more, create a loss of safety and security in the child. Even a parent's frequent work-related transfers or relocations from one school community to another can affect student learning, as does a child's being unattended when parents work long hours in or out of the home.

Barbara Oehlberg compels the reader to affirm that all children want to feel secure and protected from harm, to know that their worlds are generally predictable, and to discover and learn. When that sense of safety is undermined, the effect is compromised learning. Oehlberg expands on this basic principle by presenting research findings that reveal some startling facts. Experiencing loss, trauma, intense fear, or terror erodes a child's sense of safety and creates a physiologic effect on a child's brain function. Drawing from the work of neurologists, child development experts, and psychologists, Oehlberg provides the reader with a concise thesis: The organic effects on brain development of a child's experience involving insecurity, loss, fear, or a lack of safety can impair cognitive processing and impede learning.

She explains that students who are so affected undergo a "cognitive lock-out" and act out or withdraw from social, emotional, and learning challenges, not because they make a rational choice to do so, but because of a physiologic and emotional reaction to some feeling of fear integrated into their development. Brain research is offered to demonstrate how a student in the classroom can innocently experience a touch, smell, noise, or sight which can trigger the amygdala (a structure of the brain which directs negative human reactions to fear, arousal, and anger) to disrupt rational thought by causing a surge of adrenaline, thus invoking the fight-or-flight reaction. Additionally, the known effect of continued release of adrenaline, and its companion hormone cortisol, is loss of memory. Children who can't remember, can't learn. When students act out, they often do not know why or what triggered the conduct. Nonetheless, the general response is to apply the rules from the student code of conduct and to impose some form of punishment.

Oehlberg suggests that punishment for physiologic reactions is not the goal of learning. Rather, self-discipline and self-regulation are the aims for which education should strive; furthermore, without self-discipline and self-regulation, a student will not learn, and the larger purposes of education will be thwarted. Incumbent on the teacher is the creation of a classroom in which students feel safe. This book offers countless numbers of activities and ideas to help students become aware of their actions in order to learn to manage what is stressful and to control their reactions that detract from learning.

A safe school is one in which a student is free to take risks, to express opinions, and to be free from discrimination, fear, and shame. In order to teach children to understand their actions and reactions, educators must develop a relationship with them based on trust. Without trust, a child may regard purposeful learning challenges as threats and will act accordingly. Thus, educators must become aware of their own physiologic and emotional responses to stress.

Reaching and Teaching Stressed and Anxious Learners in Grades 4–8 is a useful tool for educators who seek to understand how increased anxiety and stress create physiologic and autonomic responses in students which interfere with learning. The author provides numerous references for the reader to explore further this important issue. This book will help the teacher create a classroom in which all students feel safe, where they can learn to express themselves in appropriate ways, and where they may develop trusting relationships with adults. The purposes of schooling are important, and the meaning of learning is profound, but without a safe place to be, the heart of the child cannot be touched, and the power of education to transform lives and our world is not possible. What lies within each child is the key to the future.

Susan G. Clark
University of Akron
Department of Educational
Foundations and Leadership

Preface

Dedicated teachers are experiencing increased dismay and frustration over mandated educational policies that focus exclusively on students' intellectual performance. Increasingly, a student's academic future is determined by a single test.

Many educators recognize that the increased pressure to perform academically is directly correlated to student acting-out behaviors, reduced motivation, and diminished hope for a fulfilling future. The alarming increase in bullying in and around schools is not surprising when considered in this context.

In our nation's economic system, students who drop out of school or receive a certificate of completion that does not equate to a graduation diploma actually become throwaways, cast aside by a society that does not want to invest in them or their futures. I find this unacceptable. The human costs of such a reality are enormous and rob our nation of the ultimate societal contributions of countless citizens. The financial costs over the next decades will be monumental.

As a retired educator, I have the opportunity to read; more specifically, I have the opportunity to read cross-disciplinary research, which has convinced me that the neurobiological literature on which this book is based holds the promise of hope for educators and students.

In my current capacity as an educational and child trauma consultant, I deliver workshops to more than 4,000 Midwest educators every year and fully appreciate their prevailing concerns over student behaviors and academic achievements. The current achievement gap that exists for many minority students is not diminishing despite concerted efforts by both teachers and youngsters. The problem is not that failing students are unable to learn; it's that our educational system does not know how to reach and teach them. The mandate of America's schools is to teach CHILDREN, not academic subjects.

The neurobiological research that serves as the foundation of this book offers insights into the complex causes of underachievement and behavioral issues. More important, it affords educators proactive solutions for these classroom, school, and community challenges.

As the academic pressures continue to mount for students, teachers, and schools, behavioral issues will increase, and academic achievements will continue to disappoint. I believe solutions will evolve out of understandings of the root causes, which are neurologically shaped by the early experiences of students, experiences over which young children have absolutely no control or choice.

The behavioral changes and developmental issues of youngsters today challenge not only educational institutions but community recreational and afterschool programs as well. The prevention of drug abuse and violence is a related issue to which the strategies of this book can be applied. Because of these broad but shared issues, this book points to current neurological research as a rationale for the featured trauma-defusing activities.

The Introduction offers a brief overview of societal shifts that have changed childhood for many youngsters. Chapter 1 provides a brief but concise explanation of recent neurological research made possible through remarkable advances in electronic imaging. Although this greatly expanded base of knowledge has been available for a decade, regrettably it has received little attention in the field of education.

The importance of enabling stressed youngsters to access their neocortex when they perceive threat is set out in Chapter 2. The implications for academic achievement and classroom climate are profound. Integrating these recommendations into school and classroom management styles is demanding because they refute so many assumptions promulgated over the years through teacher texts and training.

These opening chapters are intentionally brief to encourage busy educators and program directors to read them before going on to the specific strategies and transformative activities.

Chapter 3 offers very specific classroom activities that can alleviate the stress and perceived helplessness generated by previous losses and traumatic experiences. The activities are designed to defuse memories of fear and vulnerability through symbolic activities suited to the skills and interests of students in Grades 4–8.

By providing seed ideas for journaling, teachers furnish the metaphorical topics through which students can address and overcome the hidden barriers to their ability to focus and solve problems. Journaling offers an enriched medium for this personal and private recovery process.

Other psychomotor activities that fit into the core curriculum subjects of language arts, social studies, and history are included. Incorporating art into creative writing activities may motivate students who are less inclined to enjoy writing.

Today's youngsters are very engrossed in electronic media. This natural interest can be used to motivate students to engage in the psychomotor activity of writing, and it provides multiple advances in building resolutions, literacy skills, and personal ability to rally against perceived helplessness. Writing interview scripts for fictional radio or video programs offers multiple growth opportunities and curriculum enhancements.

The opportunities for generating resiliency in youngsters are abundant in after-school and recreational programs or clubs. Freedom from the constraints of curriculum and schedule affords favorable environments for transforming activities. Chapter 6 offers expanded activities for recovery that might not fit classroom structure.

The issue of violence prevention within schools has become significant for educators in the last decade and is the subject of Chapter 5. Elementary and middle schools have a profound opportunity to intervene in the trajectory of aggression in young students.

Recognizing the implications of the neural development of infants and children living in turbulent environments provides a new framework for violence prevention. Children who live with violence learn survival. Redirecting these innate drives requires transformation and recovery, not threats and punishments. The educational dilemma of stress buildup and the bullying epidemic that it has generated make this chapter's message more vital than ever before as schools experience changes in student behaviors, making learning and achievement uncertain.

The information in this book and its ultimate implications may seem to breach our basic understandings of the educational process as we know it. For those educators who have sensed that today's students do not seem to learn or perform in expected ways, the insights offered in the next chapters can lead to alternative strategies for generating academic achievement for students and pride and renewal for teachers.

Publisher's Acknowledgments

Corwin Press would like to thank the following reviewers for their contribution to this book:

Martha de Acosta, Director, Education and Training Programs, Milton S. Eisenhower Foundation, Shaker Heights, OH

Patricia Baker, NBCT, Elementary Gifted Education Instructor, Mary Walter Elementary School, Bealeton, VA

Gloria Avolio DePaul, NBPTS:ECYA/School Counseling, Tampa, FL

Jane Fung, Teacher, Science Center School, Los Angeles, CA

Dolores Huffman, Associate Professor of Nursing, Purdue University Calumet, School of Nursing, Hammond, IN

J. Allen Queen, Professor and Chair, Department of Educational Leadership, University of North Carolina, Charlotte, NC

Jane Sembric, Executive Director, Society for Prevention of Violence, Woodmere, OH

Janice Sedory, Fifth Grade Teacher, Limona Elementary School, Valrico, FL

Alice Smith, Ben Franklin Elementary, Grand Forks, ND

About the Author

After completing the postgraduate program in Child Development and Family Studies at the University of Akron, **Barbara Oehlberg** was employed by the Family Life Program, Office of Adult Education, Cleveland Public Schools. She wrote *Parenting for Peaceful Families: A Resource Guide for Parent Educators* for Ohio's then Governor Richard Celeste during that time.

Since retirement, Barbara has become an avid reader of neurological research and has become certified as a Child Trauma Consultant by the Institute for Trauma and Loss in Children. She serves on its board of advisers.

She has authored another book on classroom transformation of stress, preschool to Grade 3. *Making It Better: Activities for Children Living in a Stressful World* was published in 1996.

Barbara teaches continuing education unit courses for educators through Kent State and Ashland universities. She serves as a consultant for Ohio's Commission on Dispute Resolution and Conflict Management and provides inservices to Ohio's schools.

She can be reached at b.oehlberg@ameritech.net.

Many students in U.S. classrooms are painfully aware that the process of anticipated learning is not working for them. They and their teachers are bewildered and frustrated.

In recognition of their potential stress and despair, this book is dedicated to offering them the prospects of reduced anxiety, enhanced academic achievement, and a brighter future.

Introduction

Children Haven't Changed;
Childhood Has

Teachers across America are confronted daily with student behaviors they rarely encountered 15 or 20 years ago. We may have had one, possibly two, troubled and troublesome youngsters per class, but when half, or more, of a classroom contributes to repeated disruptions, our energy and patience are exhausted.

One can hear it in the teachers' lounge and read it in print: teachers are burning out and leaving the field.

While we may agree that student behaviors are distressing, insights into why this increase is occurring are numerous and vary depending on the source. Sociologists, mental health professionals, child developmentalists, and criminologists offer differing explanations. Even politicians are attempting to declare causes and create legislation to control the behaviors.

One truth is certain: no one can offer real solutions until the root causes are clarified. Furthermore, reacting to the symptoms will not generate lasting resolutions and improvements.

Societal changes that have profoundly affected childhood experiences for America's children have filtered into families and neighborhoods over the last two decades while we, the adults, were busily tending to our own children, family, and career. As we steadily developed adult coping skills, it was natural not to look back at the societal changes we had accommodated and learned to cope with.

However, the impact of these shifts on young children's sense of security and sense of connectedness significantly correlates with the behavioral changes that have so distressingly altered our roles and careers as educators. Consider the following societal changes over the past 20 years:

- Frequent images of violent, horrifying events in television news, movies, and other electronic entertainment
- Terrorists attacks within our nation
- More and more two-career families and children under one year old with mothers in the work force
- Economic shifts that prompt multiple jobs or joblessness for families

- Increasing use of alcohol and drugs, particularly crack cocaine, which can dismantle maternal behaviors and care
- More family mobility, more separation from extended families, more grandparents raising grandchildren
- More-marked concentration and isolation of poverty in urban and some rural areas
- Increases in the number of children growing up with one parent absent and the economic challenges that brings
- Increases in child abuse and neglect
- Homelessness

For many youngsters, these societal changes have altered how they see their world and how they see themselves in that world. Children growing up amid these many changes will certainly present different needs and respond to school personnel very differently from previous generations, who grew up when experiences were more predictable. Collectively these numerous changes have contributed to many, many children's deduction that adults can no longer guarantee total safety, an absolute and universal developmental requirement.

Assuredly, none of us would allow ourselves to look directly into the eyes of a youngster we care about and say, "I can assure you nothing bad is ever going to happen to you!" This reality has changed our relations with children today, whether we realize it or not. A valued and essential portion of our traditional role as adults used to be keeping children, our own and all others, safe.

Consequently, many youngsters are making adaptations, albeit maladaptations, in order to survive in an insecure world (Garbarino, 1995). It is these developmental adaptations that are generating many of the stress-driven behaviors educators encounter today. Acknowledging this correlation does not imply these behaviors are acceptable or appropriate. It does mean that if the field of education wants to reduce or eliminate them, we need to understand the root causes.

The incredible advances in electronic imaging in the past decade illuminate our understanding of the intricate timeline of brain development. For example, the research by Allan N. Schore (Solomon & Siegel, 2003) on the prefrontal cortex indicates a surge of development between eight and 12 weeks after birth. At this time the infant has the visual acuity to clearly see the facial expressions of a prime caregiver. As the caregiver mirrors and mimics the infant's facial expressions, which are often more like contortions, as they lock eyes, the adult is stimulating the infant's neural development in the prefrontal cortex during the process referred to as attachment.

The key significance of this early, early relationship experience is that the prefrontal cortex is the scaffolding on which infants build their lifetime capacity for self-regulation, for stress management, and for dealing with rapidly changing environments. The vital emotion of empathy will emanate eventually from this same area of the brain.

All of these developmental capacities are directly implicated in the student behaviors educators find most distressing and frustrating, yet the root causes began long, long before the children ever entered a school. The societal changes affecting this process of attachment point to two early relationship issues: mothers returning to the workforce soon after birth of a child and drug use interfering with the attachment process. Children have absolutely no control over these circumstances, yet their neurological circuitry bears the imprint.

Sometimes it helps to remember this remote trail of circumstances when confronted with students' belligerence and volatility. They are operating out of their prewired neurobiology. This insight does not imply the behavior should be condoned, but it does give an educator an alternative to taking it personally, a major cause of teacher burnout.

This book presents and applies valuable insights from the field of neurobiology, and readers will find neurological terminology that is not generally used in educational literature. For this reason, a glossary is included.

Glossary

The Vocabulary of
Anxiety, Stress, and Trauma

ADHD: attention-deficit/hyperactivity disorder; a neurobiological condition that inhibits youngsters from initiating self-regulatory processes that enable them to screen incoming stimuli, focus attention, and regulate physical behaviors.

Amygdala: a small part of the limbic system where memories of terror and helplessness are stored; directly involved in the adrenaline system's fight/flight/freeze reactions.

Attachment: the process of bonding and connectedness between an infant and significant care provider or parent that builds a sense of trust and security within the child.

Attachment deficits or *attachment trauma*: weak attachments that are critical in the way they impede optimal brain development and can contribute to neurological alterations, structurally and biologically.

Autonomic nervous system: same as the sensory nervous system and includes the senses, body feelings, and mind-body memories, leading to unconscious, involuntary actions and behaviors.

Bipolar disorder: extremely unstable adult behaviors, ranging from manic episodes to depressive episodes and generating grave insecurities for the children of a bipolar parent.

Brainstem: the very base of the brain, which connects with the spinal column; regulates internal physiological functioning. This part of the brain is fully operational and permanently set at birth.

Central nervous system: the conscious or cognitive thought processes that involve voluntary actions and behaviors.

Conduct disorders: a category of highly aggressive actions and risky behaviors now considered as generally trauma correlated.

Depression: a mental state of deep dejection, representing altered consciousness and brain chemistry and affecting the entire person. Behaviors range from withdrawal to aggression.

Dissociation: an involuntary, primitive defensive response of someone experiencing helplessness in stressful situations; referred to as numbing out, which allows children to survive traumatic experiences.

Electronic imaging: a category of screening that offers complex images of internal development and functioning; includes computerized axial tomography scans, positron-emission tomography scans, magnetic resonance imaging, and others.

Externalization: the process of accessing memories stored in the amygdala and bringing them into consciousness, allowing those memories to be defused, resolved, and integrated.

External memories: conscious recall when the person remembering is fully aware that he or she is remembering.

Fight/flight/freeze: involuntary reactions to perceived helplessness and terror, initiated by the adrenaline system for survival purposes.

Flashback: a body memory of a "speechless" memory from early childhood; during flashback, adults relive the traumatic experience.

Helplessness: the most significant condition and feeling generated by traumatic memories; helplessness is triggered by perceived threats unless the traumatic memory is transformed.

Hippocampus: small portions in the limbic portions of the brain, one on the left and one on the right hemisphere, that are the center of short-term memory. Neural cells within the hippocampus can be destroyed by cortisol, the hormone released during extreme stress.

Homeostasis: an internal balance that results from mind-body integration and generates a sense of calm, self-regulation, and hope.

Hyperactivity: a very visible response to stress and insecurity. In this state, traumatized children cannot focus or exercise self-regulation.

Hypersensitivity: an acute state of anxiety. In this state, children are easily triggered by their sensory interpretations of stressors and stimulations.

Hypervigilance: an acute state of anxiety. In this state, children are easily triggered by their sensory interpretations of fears, threats, and danger.

Implicit memories: internal or body memories that are triggered involuntarily and during which youngsters are *not* aware they are remembering.

Intrusive thoughts: unbidden thoughts and images generated involuntarily by the sensory nervous system of traumatized children. Intrusive thoughts interfere with children's ability to focus.

Limbic system: area deep within the brain, referred to as the Grand Central Station for emotions. It includes the amygdala and hippocampus plus other segments.

Midbrain: area of the brain between the limbic system and brainstem. It is the Grand Central Station for determining safety and security and is quite fully developed by three or three and one half years of age, after which its malleability begins to diminish.

Mind-body memories: whole-body memories, which include sensory and intellectual or psychological reminders. Traumatic memories are mind-body memories that trigger stress overloads.

Neocortex: the rippled overlay portion of the brain, referred to as the new brain; affords humans the development of language, abstract thought, and problem resolution. It remains malleable throughout life.

Neural integration: the full and free flow of sensory and cortical information, allowing the individual to make fully informed, rational behavioral decisions.

Neurobiological alterations: structural and chemical changes in brain development, which can result from living in stressful and persistently threatening environments; often made for survival purposes.

Numbing: the survival responses in children that allow them to dissociate and not be fully conscious of overwhelmingly frightening experiences.

Posttraumatic stress disorder (PTSD): a condition that can result from witnessing violence or experiencing sudden, shocking fear and horror that overwhelms one's capacity to cope.

Prefrontal cortex: area of the brain just under the neocortex and behind the eyes; referred to as the brain's executive manager. One of its significant duties in the process of self-regulation is to monitor and regulate the reactions of the amygdala to perceived threats. Infants not afforded optimal attachment opportunities can experience an underdeveloped prefrontal cortex, resulting in weakened capacities for self-control, stress management, and empathy.

Psychomotor activities: activities that engage the sensory nervous system through hand and/or body movement.

Regression: the unconscious and involuntary process that results in a youngster's reverting to an earlier behavior that had brought the child comfort.

Self-regulation: the internal capacity to exercise self-control and personal behavioral management through optimal neurological development and functioning.

Sensory nervous system: includes the autonomic nervous system, involving involuntary responses to information generated by the five senses.

Shocking losses: sudden, horrific losses that generate difficult grieving and can be perceived by a youngster as a traumatic experience.

Somatic: relating to the body; a physical sensation or body response.

State of anxiety: the triggered mental state of extreme stress and helplessness that causes a child to automatically downshift out of the neocortex for survival purposes.

Threats: words and/or actions that are perceived to be or are actual intentions by another to injure; include physical, emotional, intellectual, psychological, social, racial, or resource threats.

Transformation: the process of defusing and externalizing encoded memories of fear and helplessness, thereby disarming the memory.

Trauma: a frightening, unpredictable experience of fear and instability that can be perceived as life threatening. The effects of trauma on a child are determined by the age and developmental stage of the child, by whether the trauma was singular or repetitive, and by whether it was inflicted by a person the child needs to trust or by a stranger. How care providers or significant adults respond to the child and the event will also determine how the child interprets its severity.

Triggers: the sensory stimuli that initiate involuntary autonomic or physical reactions to memories of fear and helplessness, regardless of the time elapsed since the event.

Part I

Brain Changes and How They Affect Student Behaviors and Learning

1

The Impact of Losses and Stress on the Student's Mind and Body

I t may seem to be an irony that in a wealthy nation, many children are confronted with loss; compounding the irony, children face losses that adults seemingly navigate with ease. However, significant losses are cumulative and can change a child's understanding of self and even alter brain development.

LOSSES

In every classroom there are students who have experienced grievous losses within their immediate circumstances. For some, these losses have been multiple; for some, they have been sudden and shocking. Understandably, shocking losses mean the family is also in crisis, and the grieving adult(s) may not be able to fully attend to their hurting 9- to 14-year-old.

James Fogarty tells us, in his book *The Magical Thoughts of Grieving Children* (2000), that youngsters in concrete operations (ages 7 to 11) are still able to engage in magical thinking, much as they did as preschoolers. Generating explanations that help youngsters understand something over which they have had no control brings them temporary relief. Magical thinking is a natural way of coping with the realization that one was helpless and couldn't bring about a more desirable ending.

As students developmentally move out of concrete operations, they become painfully aware of deeper understandings of injustices and unfulfilled needs in their lives. Among the experiences that now need processing and integration might be the death of their parents' marriage, or divorce (Fogarty), and the fact that one of their parents has chosen *not* to participate in their young life—losses often assumed to have been left behind.

However, when children languish in "if only . . ." thinking and assume accountability for a tragic incident in order to shield themselves from a sense of helplessness, they are *not* processing their grief. When unresolved losses collide with prepubescent hormones, that unresolved grief can explode into anger and rage. Aggressive or acting-out behaviors generally follow.

Fogarty demonstrated that anger is not a primary feeling but an umbrella or cover for the following feelings of despair and fear resulting from those unresolved losses:

1. The sense of abandonment, resulting from such events as divorce, parents in prison, placement in foster care or with a grandparent, adoption, or one parent's choosing not to parent

2. The sense of betrayal, resulting from having been treated as invisible or given explanations one now recognizes as less than the total truth

3. The sense of helplessness, resulting from witnessing domestic violence or realizing one was powerless to prevent or stop a loss or tragic situation

4. The sense of shame, the result of perceiving that the grievous loss or unfulfilled needs mean one was unlovable

5. The sense of hopelessness, resulting from feelings that nothing will ever change or get better

6. The sense of disappointment, from grief over promises not kept and assurances not fulfilled

7. Sadness or depression, a blend of all of the above, resulting in no desire to continue

While these feelings emerge out of perceptions or interpretations, not realities, the feelings are very real to youngsters and ultimately drive their behaviors, that is, until the feelings are transformed, as described in Chapter 2. The inappropriate behaviors cannot be resolved until the children have had an opportunity to symbolically process and integrate their loss.

Young people of previous generations certainly experienced grievous losses and yet presented less volatile behaviors. It is natural to ponder why today's children can't just "suck it up" and "get over it," as the vernacular of earlier times might put it. Instead, we need to realize that we are in a society in which the cumulative changes in childhood collide with circumstances (such as parents' divorce) to exacerbate a child's affect and acting-out behaviors.

The challenge for the field of education and the community is whether to continue to react to the symptoms or instead to respond to the causes.

STRESS

The relationship issues outlined in the Introduction, stemming from attachment trauma, can overly sensitize youngsters to stress and result in stress pileups (Allen, 2001). When traumas collide with current stress, a student's underdeveloped prefrontal cortex may not be able to maintain a state of self-regulation. The student is then propelled into an unbearably painful emotional state of anxiety. Such stress pileup can generate the destructive actions of aggression, violence, and rage. It can also lead to self-destructive actions and depression. These are not simply moral issues or character flaws but the results of early relationship issues.

Experiencing abuse or neglect during infancy, as a toddler, or as a preschooler similarly affects the areas of the brain engaged in primal development at those stages. The neurobiological research by Bruce D. Perry reveals that young children living in persistently unpredictable and unsafe environments experience altered brain development for survival purposes. The midbrain and limbic systems of children who live with insecurity become hardwired for detecting threats to their well-being. Any real or perceived threat initiates an instant fight/flight/freeze reaction. Survival is a prime value, not a choice (Karr-Morse & Wiley, 1997). This built-in wiring of the alarm system will be operational in students in Grades 4–8 if no trauma transformation has been achieved.

Such traumatic memories of fear and helplessness are not cognitively available to the student; however, the behavioral reactions to threats and insecurities become real—to the student and to all others in the school setting.

WHEN TRAUMATIC MEMORIES ARE TRIGGERED

Very young children naturally dissociate, or numb out, when traumatic memories are triggered. Because such very early memories are body memories (Rothschild, 2000) rather than verbal memories, words and cognitive expressions are not possible for the traumatized child. The only way the youngster can express the triggered fear and insecurity is through actions, survival actions that appear to others as acting up and hyperactivity. The brain wiring resulting from very early childhood experiences of insecurity and unpredictability constitutes a developmental alteration in the brain, not what may be known as posttraumatic stress disorder. These brain changes become the tragic legacy of students who have had early childhood traumas.

However, with the onset of puberty, males make a dramatic shift from dissociation to aggression, or survival actions that appear to others as violent and assaultive. One explanation links this aggression to the anthropological male role of hunter and protector. This explanation does not address the current presentation of aggression in girls, however.

As with the issue of loss, the significant increases in volatile classroom behaviors reflect the combined effects of early stressful life experiences and living in a turbulent world. Witnessing domestic violence is particularly devastating and is now recognized as a major contributing factor in preadolescent rage (Bloom & Reichert, 1998). Young children cannot run away or leave the dwelling; neither can they predict when domestic violence might erupt. Consequently, they live in a constant state of helplessness, only to explode when threatened by anyone, often at school.

The stunning insight for teachers made possible through this recent neurological research is that students who experienced insecure childhoods are unable to access the neocortex when in a state of anxiety. This illumination makes the topics of stress, loss, and trauma relevant educational issues. My experience has been that when they receive this information, teachers express dismay over why it has not been integrated into educational policy or teacher training.

COGNITIVE LOCKOUT

The cognitive lockout notion not only offers an understanding of increases in student hyperactivity and aggression but opens the door for explanations for the underachievement of alarming numbers of America's students. With the increased pressures and penalties of the No Child Left Behind Act now trickling down to local schools, I can only hope these cross-discipline topics are added to the conversation.

Unfortunately, without full integration of this vital information, more and more of America's children will be left behind, locked out, and literally thrown away.

Once again, early relationships and attachment trauma come into play. When an infant's prefrontal cortex is not stimulated into optimal development, its capacity to modulate the limbic system is diminished and self-regulation is weakened. Later, when that youngster or adolescent senses threat or danger, the limbic system, through the amygdala, virtually hijacks the monitoring capability of the underdeveloped prefrontal cortex. When this happens, the brain downshifts in a state of anxiety, and the survival-driven behaviors of volatile aggression erupt (see Figure 1.1).

When in this anxiety-driven survival mode, the brain has downshifted *out* of the neocortex, eliminating any possibility of engaging in problem-solving. This involuntary process is referred to as cognitive lockout. The midbrain and limbic system cannot engage in the learning process; only the neocortex can (Bailey, 2000). The neocortex is the only area of the brain where a choice can be made, that is, where rationality and logic can operate.

Figure 1.1   Brain Areas Discussed in This Book

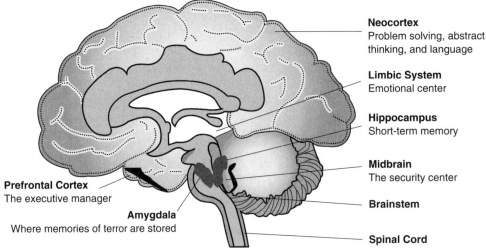

Neocortex
Problem solving, abstract thinking, and language

Limbic System
Emotional center

Hippocampus
Short-term memory

Midbrain
The security center

Brainstem

Spinal Cord

Prefrontal Cortex
The executive manager

Amygdala
Where memories of terror are stored

Furthermore, when in a state of anxiety, the brain cannot recall information processed and stored successfully during less stressful times. This limits the student's ability to demonstrate successful learning—and successful teaching. Test taking becomes an intimidating nightmare for such a student. Proficiency tests are interpreted by these students to be an intellectual threat, and so these tests elevate the students' state of anxiety. In today's climate, a student's impaired test taking becomes a peril for the student's teacher, principal, and school as well as the student.

For a student who is the child of attachment trauma and a chaotic home environment, cognitive lockout also blocks the capability to participate in personal safety. For these students, deducing how to avoid future occurrences of threatening harm is not possible because they cannot learn from what they cannot remember. This means they live in perpetual helplessness and vulnerability; hence they rely on hypersensitivity and hypervigilance. Debate is growing over the clear differentiation between these hyperactive behaviors resulting from trauma on the one hand and attention-deficit/hyperactivity disorder, conduct disorder, and bipolar disorder on the other. The significance of assessments and interventions is pronounced for educators, parents, and students (Breggin, 2000; Fogarty, 2000; Silva, 2004).

Not only are these youngsters unable to control their volatile behaviors; they have no control over their emotional turbulence. Involuntary memories of terror are triggered by sensory arousals: by sounds, sights, aromas, touches, or movements that occur naturally and repeatedly around them. Hearing a siren somewhere outside the school building will undoubtedly trigger flashbacks of some crisis for individual students in a classroom.

These sensory triggers go unnoticed by peers or adults but terrorize the student with an unresolved trauma or insecurities from early childhood. Even more debilitating for traumatized students, remembering the incident of a terrorizing triggered flashback is also denied them because that memory is stored in the amygdala, *not* in their neocortex. These terrorizing sensations are beyond any internal controls, and life becomes a living nightmare. Such flashbacks or intrusive sensations make concentration and the ability to focus tenuous, if not impossible.

It is also possible for students from stable, supportive families to experience traumatic stress and cognitive lockout resulting from singular frightening events, such as natural disasters or being chased by a dog. Fortunately, recovery is more easily achieved for them when transforming activities and interventions are introduced.

Singular shocking experiences, such as car accidents, house fires, a surgical or health crisis, or witnessing or experiencing an assault or rape, can overwhelm a youngster's capacity to cope. Even learning about a shocking incident happening to a peer or relative can generate similar stress in some youngsters. There is no way to predict who will be affected and who will not (Steele, 1998).

The terrorist attacks of September 11, 2001, and the incessant television news images that followed, traumatized students across America. Unfortunately, shocking events happen quite regularly, locally, nationally, and internationally.

The confusing aspect of singular or secondhand traumatic stress for educators is that the dramatic behavioral changes often are not presented for months, possibly for more than a year, after the event. Only when the youngster feels totally safe will the numbing begin to subside. Unfortunately, the adults in that student's life have moved beyond recalling the event, and the student may be with a different teacher. Consequently, no one connects the sudden distressing behaviors, so inconsistent with previous patterns, with the tragic event so far in the past (Terr, 1990).

Regrettably, because there appears to be no logical reason for these new behaviors, they are declared a discipline issue and treated as such by school policy.

Finally, a lasting devastation, for the students and their teachers, of living in persistently threatening environments is the destructive effect of the stress hormone cortisol on the neural cells in the hippocampus. The hippocampus is the center of memory in the human brain. This tragedy is another example of how environments and experiences affect academic achievements far more than genetics do (Bremner, 2002).

INTERVENTIONS ARE POSSIBLE

Certainly the safety and security within the school community will have an impact on the levels of loss and stress of the students in attendance. Hopefully, the information offered in this chapter will make it possible for educators to gain insights into the reasons for distressing student behaviors, permitting teachers to understand that these behaviors are not a personal affront. Securing parental input regarding any out-of-the-ordinary family happenings may also help teachers understand student behavior changes.

Take hope: the neurological and behavioral changes that have developed are not permanent in students in Grades 4–8—not yet. Specific strategies and activities for transforming and healing begin in Chapter 2.

2

Regaining
Cognitive Access

The Process of Transforming Stress and the Sense of Helplessness

Reaching and teaching youngsters living in a turbulent world is a very different educational process from what we as teachers experienced during our own latency years. Stressed students' process of learning probably differs greatly from the process suited to the educational strategies we were taught during our undergraduate teaching courses and any subsequent training.

To change one's pattern of teaching is uncomfortable and challenging, especially if it worked—or used to. Most teachers chose this profession because it offered an opportunity to make a real difference in the lives of children. Generating that sense of accomplishment is getting more and more difficult for many of us. The underlying reasons that make reaching some students so frustrating are not a direct reflection of teacher commitment; nevertheless, changing one's teaching style is hardly a welcome concept. However, experiencing success is tremendously fulfilling to professional teachers. The balance of this book contains suggestions and student activities that will enhance that possibility.

TRANSFORMING PERCEPTIONS OF HELPLESSNESS

As outlined in the previous chapter, environmental and relational experiences can cause neurobiological alterations that become barriers to cognitive learning. Because confusing and frightening memories are *not* stored in the neocortex or central nervous system, caring adults cannot erase them in children through rational discussion and intellectual dialogue. Students cannot resolve the mysteries of their intrusive and debilitating sensations of fright by being told not to worry or to just get past it (Rothschild, 2000).

Because these unbidden memories are stored within the amygdala, a part of the sensory nervous system, the only way a youngster can unlock them is through a psychomotor action or activity. Shocking memories are implicit, or nonconscious, and the child is not aware of remembering them. Instead, the experience is more like reliving the incident unknowingly (Allen, 2001).

However, youngsters have to access the internal memory before they can confront and resolve it. Sensory activities permit children to connect with the overwhelming memory in order to externalize the imprint of terror and helplessness and overcome it. Symbolic psychomotor activities make it possible for youngsters to begin to manage the memory instead of the memory's managing them.

A recent study of how school-based intervention that focuses on trauma and grief improves academic achievement for middle school students was conducted by William Saltzman, Robert Pynoos, and colleagues (Saltzman, Pynoos, Layne, Heinberg, & Aisenberg, 2001). The journaling and drawing interventions described in this report were led by a highly qualified team from the University of California, Los Angeles, and offer encouraging results for public education.

Unfortunately, financial and professional resources of this caliber are not available for the schools with large numbers of students exposed to shocking losses and traumas. The persistent demands for increased student achievement challenge schools to consider alternative ways to provide similar opportunities to stressed and grieving students.

Participating in any form of the arts automatically provides this essential opportunity to externalize the frozen, unconscious memory of helplessness that may be literally locked in the student's mind-body memory system. These are the memories that can shut down the learning process (Steele, 1999).

Creative writing and journaling are productive psychomotor activities that fit naturally into already crowded elementary and middle school curriculums. Suggesting the creation of illustrations or cartoons that could accompany a story enhances the potential for a transformation of the troubled memory.

Providing anxious youngsters with an opportunity to create story endings that transform a powerless character into one of strength vicariously empowers the students to privately, internally move forward to survival, which permits them to embrace a sense of security and future. Classroom teachers can provide anxious students with the tools for generating academic resiliency and building coping skills for living in a troubling world (Brohl & Diaz, 1995).

By providing students with a chance to melt an internal blockage to their neocortex and ultimately trust their ability to problem solve again, teachers give them an opportunity to become self-motivated. Without actually realizing that a breakthrough has taken place, the student is freed to become a more active learner. Reducing the likelihood of having their debilitating sensory memories triggered by the sound of a siren or a loud, sudden clap reduces stress, and the student is freed to engage in energized intellectual explorations (Rothschild, 2000).

Adding yet another issue for teachers and schools with an already overburdened schedule may seem unthinkable. However, the promise of reducing teacher frustration and stress while recovering time lost to behavioral issues puts trauma recovery strategies into a more inviting framework. Generating academic successes can reduce stress and renew both educators and students.

Classroom teachers are not expected to be clinicians or therapists, nor should they be. However, educators are under greater pressure than ever before to increase the academic achievement of students, particularly those students who are struggling and underachieving. Many of these are the same youngsters whose learning could be bolstered by strategies and activities presented in the remaining chapters of this book. These are also the youngsters who will probably never have access to the services of a clinician or therapist to help them reach their full, genetic potential.

As teachers, we can choose to integrate transforming activities into classroom schedules at least once a week. Additional activities might be considered when one of the students is dealing with a new crisis that the teacher is aware of. The reasons for such specialized activities would not be disclosed by the teacher because the entire class participates.

Of course, teachers are not qualified to interpret or assign meanings to creative writings or drawings of students unless they have participated in specialized training for counselors or social workers. Equally critical is the necessity to respect students' confidentiality and privacy.

As mandated reporters of child abuse, however, teachers must pass on to the appropriate authorities any information that suggests such abuse.

STRENGTHENING SELF-REGULATION

Interpersonal neurobiology (Solomon & Seigel, 2003), the process whereby nurturing relationships become the virtual architect of the brain, was outlined in Chapter 1. Through the capacity of the prefrontal right lobe to regulate the autonomic nervous system, which includes the amygdala, children can maintain homeostasis and avert downshifting out of the neocortex. Self-regulation capacities are built in early childhood and define a person's lifelong ability to manage stress.

Neural integration permits mind-body self-regulation when the mind is aware of what the body is doing. When anxiety propels the amygdala to hijack the regulatory capacities of the prefrontal cortex, young people's behaviors tend to become hyper, outside of regulation, or outside of self-control. When the amygdala is triggered, the student has lost mind-body integration; the mind is not aware of what the body is doing (Bailey, 2000; Greenwald, 2002).

In a recent workshop for educators, a teacher literally gasped with an "aha!" as I explained the process of temporarily lost mind-body integration. She quickly asked whether that's why students insist they haven't done a particular action when teachers saw it with their own eyes.

This is probably the most challenging aspect of accepting the full implications of current neurological research. As that teacher and I processed her new understanding further, she repeated a misconception I hear frequently: when students deny engaging in an unacceptable action, they are trying to see what they can get away with.

In such situations, the traditional deduction that the student is deliberately lying becomes an added label clouding the incident. To understand that the student's mind is not cognitively aware of what he or she has just done while in a state of anxiety is not to condone the behavior. Instead, such an awareness can provide the framework through which both student and educator can proceed toward a resolution and an alternative or learned behavior change.

According to Becky Bailey (2000), our job as teachers is to make it possible for the prefrontal lobes to regulate the lower portion of the brain, from which survival reactions to stress and fears emanate.

The brain operates optimally when it senses it is safe. Adults can provide verbal assurances that enhance such perceptions. Teachers can use mentoring communications that enable an anxious student to return to his neocortex following a stressful experience that has propelled a downshift into the limbic system and midbrain. When students are *not* operating out of their neocortex, they cannot choose their behaviors. Neither can they actively participate in problem solving and the learning process, including learning more acceptable behaviors.

The clues to a student's state of mind can be interpreted from his or her behaviors, providing adults with a guide for a proactive response. Students who have downshifted into their emotional center, their limbic system, present behavioral cues that include name-calling and other verbal abuse. By using empathy and mirroring what we heard, we as teachers can help the youngsters become aware of their emotional state. In such situations, we can increase their sense of security by responding, "You seem very upset. You had hoped to use that computer now. It's very hard for you when you're feeling that way. What can the two of you do to work this out?"

Students engaged in the physical actions of punching or kicking have downshifted into the survival center within their midbrain and brainstem. We adults can ease the student back into the neocortex by describing what we see, thereby helping the youngster's mind become aware of the actions the body has engaged in. "I saw your hand form a fist." To declare a behavioral judgment about the behavior in such a situation would exacerbate the youngster's sense of insecurity and shut down the opportunity to enhance self-regulation skills.

Developing the student's self-awareness stimulates the regulatory capacity of the frontal lobes; guilt and shame do not. A productive response might be, "Hitting is not a safe thing to do. I can't let you hit him. It's my job to keep everyone safe, and your job is to help keep it that way."

Admittedly, these are not communications that would come easily for us when we are operating out of our limbic system or midbrain. During stressful times, teachers can easily get "hooked" by a student's behavior, only to discover we ourselves have been triggered into downshifting, making it unlikely that we could choose our response. In other words, we find ourselves reacting. When adults lose self-control, according to Bailey (2000), we reinforce the very behaviors in our students that we need to modify or eliminate.

Depending on how successfully we have processed our own memories of childhood, we may be inclined to rationalize that threats worked when we were youngsters and that teachers would be shirking their duty if they let the student get away with unacceptable behaviors.

Describing the behaviors we see and verbalizing empathy does not mean we condone unacceptable actions. Neither are we declaring them acceptable. We are reframing the scenario as an opportunity to strengthen students' ability to self-regulate. We are mentoring them toward resolutions that lead to advantages for them, the entire class, and ourselves. We are declaring that emotional safety in this classroom is a priority.

A teacher in a workshop reported this experience: A day after the teacher had responded to unsafe behaviors by sixth-grade students in the classroom, a male student approached while the teacher was listing assignment pages on the board. While standing behind her, he quietly asked, "How did you know?"

She replied, "Know what?" to which he responded, "How did you know I don't know where I can feel safe?" A very personal conversation followed. Later, the teacher learned he was being bullied and had never reported the bullying to anyone.

It would be ideal if all students came to school with a well-developed capacity for self-regulation. Through no fault of their own, more and more youngsters do not seem to have these abilities. The window of opportunity for developing them is brief and may be closing by the middle school years. As educators, we can nurture and model these important life skills.

By strengthening students' capacities for self-regulation, educators can increase the likelihood that academically at-risk youngsters will be able to transform memories of fear and helplessness. Such recovery holds the best promise for producing the academic achievement that teachers and administrators are being pressured to generate and be accountable for.

A story that depicts exceptional success in reframing behavior was shared by a teacher in a course I teach for continuing education units. This teacher taught all-day kindergarten. Her room was next to the school's multipurpose room, which served as the cafeteria.

A fourth-grade boy was universally identified as the worst bully in the entire school. When he was in the lunchroom, the entire room was in chaos. Since the teacher's kindergarten students took their trays into her classroom to eat, the principal asked if this particular boy could spend his lunch period in her room the rest of the year.

When there was a knock on the door of her room at noon the next day, the teacher was prepared. She welcomed the fourth grader with a clipboard and the following words: "I've been asking since school began for an assistant teacher, and here you are—welcome!" She had listed several tasks on the clipboard, from which he chose to work with the nine students who hadn't yet mastered tying their shoestrings. Within two weeks, they were accomplished at the task.

Despite being a very poor reader, he read stories to her students over the lunch hour. Her students loved every minute.

This phenomenal behavior change did not extend to any other students or places within the building or outside. When the kindergarten students met him in the halls, however, they ran to him and hugged him, while all the other students walked as close to the hall perimeters as possible.

The teacher learned on the last day of school that, unfortunately, the boy was about to move, not for the first time, and would be in another school the next year.

This example demonstrates the dramatic changes in students' behavior that can be achieved simply by a teacher's not threatening but instead connecting students to their inner potential when they feel valued and safe.

Providing a learning sanctuary for students is not an easy task when so many of them bring hypersensitivity and hypervigilance to school with them. Adding to this stress is the pressure, on both student and teacher, for academic achievement.

In addition to building trusting relationships with students, teachers can provide classroom activities that are integrated into core curriculum subjects and that at the same time symbolically defuse and transform stress and anxiety, as Chapter 3 outlines.

Part II

Activities for Transforming the Helplessness Generated by Stress and Fear

3

Language Arts

Creative Writing and Journaling

L anguage arts is the core curriculum area that provides a natural fit for assignments or activities that can help transform memories of fear and helplessness. Assigning creative writing or journaling topics with which students can hone writing skills at the same time as they anonymously address intrinsic issues that block full cortical engagement can provide empowering experiences for academically at-risk students (Corder & Brohl, 1996). The students for whom these healing activities may be the most helpful will not be aware of their need. Neither will they realize that a transformation may have occurred following the activity, but their teachers will notice a shift in behaviors and learning.

It is imperative that these topics afford symbolic correlations to helplessness and *not* be so direct that they trigger a retraumatization of students. For that reason, the suggested topics need to be hypothetical situations involving an imaginary person. The goal is to avert any chance that students will downshift out of their neocortex. Internalized perceptions of helplessness would be reinforced, not resolved, should a topic or issue result in a student's being locked out of the problem-solving capacity of the neocortex.

The greater the level of personal choice and creative flexibility in the writing guidelines, the greater the chance that students will develop a story line that provides them with symbolic relief and empowerment. Relaxing grammar and spelling evaluations, at least temporarily, will enhance the potential for deeper transforming experiences.

Creative writing permits youngsters to reach deep inside, to the places where their fears and loneliness hide. This psychomotor process enables students to hear their own voices and find their personal truth. Creative writing allows them to connect with the powerful possibilities of their dreams, and their lives take on new meaning through a newfound belief in themselves, along with a validation of their hurts and needs. The words they write can serve as a magic mirror, reflecting who they are and who they want to be and can be.

Writing about the wrongs in one's community, society, or nation is empowering to students. It allows them to look at issues from different perspectives as they begin to formulate their own beliefs, according to research by Caryn Mirriam Goldberg (1999). Through the process of externalizing their deductions and beliefs, implanted by the experiences they have had or missed out on, they can begin to remove the barriers and sense that they can give something of value to the world.

In her book *Write Where You Are,* Goldberg suggests students begin with an interview with themselves 20 years from now. What would they ask themselves? What would they be most proud of? What might be their wishes and regrets at that time? How might the world look to them then?

Be prepared to protect the confidentiality of your students and their vulnerabilities. The creative writing and art produced through the activities outlined here must not be evaluated by the guidelines in zero-tolerance admonitions.

Furthermore, to avoid a conflict between the roles of mentor and mandated reporter, you can suggest to students that they can decide if a journaling entry is to remain private and unread by the teacher by folding the page(s) halfway over.

Creative writing and journaling topics are presented below according to the primary issues they could be symbolically applied to. Feel free to develop your own expanded educational activities or projects that could reinforce the overall experience. Depending on your available class time and resources, decide how extensive such projects might be. Connecting your class with a class in a lower grade or a community or local governmental agency for project enrichment can be very meaningful. Hurting youngsters can vicariously heal themselves when they give or provide a way for other hurting children to get what they themselves never had a chance to receive.

TOPICS FOR CREATIVE WRITING AND JOURNALING

The topics are grouped under six main issues:

1. Issues of loss and being lost or invisible

2. Issues of rejection or being excluded

3. Issues of brokenness, helplessness, or futurelessness

4. Issues of betrayals or broken promises

5. Issues of emotional intelligence (dealing with feelings)

6. Issues of hope, empowerment, and healing

Issues of Loss and Being Lost or Invisible

An alien from outer space who has created for himself or herself a human face that always smiles. No one realizes the alien is miserable and very lonely. Also, the alien needs foods not available on earth but never says so.

A prince who never listens to his subjects or pays any attention to their requests or needs.

A house that can talk and tell the story of what it has seen and what it wishes could be different.

A young Native American who has found a way to make shoes or sandals that have the ability to make adults walk in children's shoes and sense their hurts, loneliness, or invisibility. Expand on how this changes the lives of children.

A child who has found a bottle containing a potion that can make people invisible. Where or when does the child give the potion to others, and what are the results ?

An artist who has the ability to paint the hidden longings and true inner needs of her portrait subjects. What happens when the friends or relatives see these truths in the finished portraits? How are relationships changed?

A youngster who can make masks that actually change the personalities of the people the child gives them to. Who would he make masks for, and how would they be changed? Or would he make one for himself, and what changes in his life would he experience?

A school bag designed to provide support, strength, and encouragement to students changing schools. How might it be most helpful, and what differences might it make?

Issues of Rejection or Being Excluded

A dog that was rejected by a neighborhood pack of dogs he wants to join.

A robot or toy stamped "defective" at the factory.

An abandoned house that is occupied by broken dreams. What does it do to make itself inviting when a young family walks down the street looking for a home?

A race car and driver who were rejected from a race because the car was painted the wrong color.

An elephant that was moved to a different zoo. The three elephants that were there refused to greet or touch her and always turned in the opposite direction.

A clown who was not applauded by the audience because he or she looked and acted too sad.

A puppy, whose mother became ill and could no longer provide adequate milk, was taken to another house with a nursing female and a litter of pups. The litter never allowed the new puppy to nurse; two of them always chased the puppy away.

Issues of Brokenness, Helplessness, or Futurelessness

A magical Band-Aid that has the ability to heal any hurt it is applied to. Where would it be applied, and what might result from the healing?

A machine that can't be turned off. What happens?

A toolbox that can be used to fix the world. What tools would be inside, and how would the world be changed?

An elderly lady who provides her community with a hospital for dolls and teddy bears. How might the community and its children be changed?

A space cadet who is on a spaceship that falls into a black hole. What does the cadet think and do to regain hope?

A puppy that wants to be a loving puppy in a litter of angry, rough-and-tumble puppies. Elaborate.

A child at summer camp who is having severe stomach pains but doesn't tell anyone. Elaborate.

A youngster who finds pieces of broken dreams on the beach and puts them back together like pieces of a puzzle. How might this lead to changes in the child?

Animals dealing with panic and how they shake it off. Pick an animal: an elk, a bear, or a coyote.

A child who finds a hawk or falcon with a broken wing. How might this lead to changes in the child?

A rancher who trained young horses by whipping them. A young Native American demonstrated to the rancher how to break a young horse by looking it in the eyes and developing trust.

Issues of Betrayal or Broken Promises

A scientist who discovered a formula or recipe for ink that would become invisible when mistruths were written. Elaborate on how or where this might lead to changes in a community.

A tree in the park that could detect when a promise was being made by someone sitting on the park bench beneath it. When the promise maker had no intention of keeping the promise, the tree would flutter and wave its branches frantically. How might this bring about changes in the community? What kinds of changes?

Describe a suitcase that could be used to pack away promises not kept. Who would own this suitcase, and how would it change the person's life?

A homeless man who had a young dog for a companion. One day the man became very angry, which resulted in the dog's being seriously injured. Describe the man's feelings about what he had done, and tell what he did to make things better for the dog and himself.

Issues of Emotional Intelligence (Dealing With Feelings)

Write as many ways as possible that a tree could symbolically describe feelings and emotional states or attitudes. Consider all the different parts of a tree: roots, trunk, branches, leaves, and fruit.

A community elder who has the ability to hear with the heart. Elaborate on how this would contribute to the community and bring about changes.

A drum (African or Native American) that has the ability to be heard only by people who are hurting and sad and lonely. How might the listeners be changed?

A child who has the ability to feel in colors. How might this gift be helpful to other children in the community?

A tummy ache or headache that can talk. What might it say, and how could this help other children?

A toolbox children could use to manage their feelings. What tools would be inside? Describe how they would work on which feelings. What changes would be made?

A lunch box that can provide food for the soul. What foods are inside, and how might they energize feelings? Which feelings?

How taking a trip or journey could be similar in a symbolic way to dealing with feelings. Include different types of transportation, a variety of terrains or roads, and the feelings that match.

A guitar that can be heard only by sad children. Its music is so inviting that children can't resist, only to discover they are no longer sad. Describe how the guitar music was able to change the children's feelings and how they acted.

Taming the beast of rage.

Issues of Hope, Empowerment, and Healing

A homeless person who gives seeds to children for "flowers of hope."

An elderly man in an old truck who provides cans of paint and paintbrushes to youngsters in a neighborhood. How are the children changed and the neighborhood altered after the painting is completed?

A river in Africa that is reported to have magical healing waters. Elaborate on who changes and how changes result.

A mask that can change to become whatever identity the person wearing it needs to be in different settings or locations. Elaborate.

A youngster who travels through space and discovers a new planet that is habitable. Describe the type of community the child would set up.

A Boy Scout troop on a mountain hike finds a very dirty, ragged boy about six years old who would not or could not speak. What would the boys in the troop decide was important to give to or introduce to the boy they found? How would they treat the boy and insist others treat him?

A scientist who has been successful in developing a pill that can cure children's memories of fear and being shamed. Who would the scientist give the pills to, and how would those people be changed?

A pair of magical glasses that can change the reality of what an adult or child sees. Who would you want to give those glasses to, and how would those people be changed?

A person called the "Ambassador of Dreams" comes to a neighborhood one summer. Who would seek this person's advice, and how would they be changed?

Capturing the asthma panther.

Confining the asthma tornado.

Harnessing the allergy alligator.

Training the diabetes dinosaur.

Conquering the test monster.

Debating Points and Issues

Sustaining students' commitment to learning, especially those already sliding into alienation, requires an education that brings meaning to their life and the world they experience daily. The struggle for survival that has to take precedence in so many young lives demands that the topics discussed and the information gleaned relate realistically to their world in order for them to motivate themselves and be open to learning.

Many students living in destabilized neighborhoods sense that getting a public school education cannot guarantee their survival or safe passage into adulthood. Troubled youth need to understand their past, integrate it into their understandings of the present, and utilize that energy and knowledge to shape their future.

Another format for addressing community or societal issues that may have become barriers to empowerment for students is preparing debating points. Suggest students compile eight to 10 points for and against the issues of their choice and describe their reasoning. Here are some possible issues:

Using the Confederate flag as a school logo

Adjudicating 14-year-olds as adults

Giving voting rights to 16-year-olds

Removing children from parent(s) because of poverty or homelessness

Taking away prisoners' right to vote

Reducing immigration

Increasing gun control

Registering as a pacifist by age 15

Strengthening controls or regulations over television advertising directed at children

"Nesting" (children remain in the family home, and the divorced parents take weekly turns in residence)

Prose and Poetry

Rhythm and cadence automatically provide a deep resonance with hidden memories and the emotions they evoke. Students can find that creating prose and poetry connects with internal energies in surprisingly powerful ways. The metaphorical associations or meanings may remain hidden, but the sense of relief can be very rejuvenating.

The following topics are offered as suggestions. Select and change them in accordance with the grade and maturity of your students:

Pain Drain

Cancer Dancer

Visitation
    Hesitation

Stompin' Out Hate

Stompin' Out Fear

Father Hunger

Pet Abuse

Fatherhood

Pit Bulls

The Security Beat

The Safety Rap

Hate Baiting

Clique Sense

Gang Proofing

Bully Proofing

Curfews

Race Baiting

Safe Gangs

Betrayal Beat

Communication
    Domination

Family Fixer

Emotion Devotion

Fences

Separation
    Declaration

Kids' Rights

Orphan Morphin'

Connection Detection

Betrayal Sensational

Blaming/Shaming

Dance of Denial

Memory Tangle

Throwaway Kids

Unloading Baggage

Rumor Machine

Sarcasm Busters

Being in My
    Own Power

Badges of Pain

Flood of Feelings

Safe Bathrooms

The Black Hole
    of Feelings

Emotional Tornados

Rivers of Rage

Rainbows of Hope

Queen Bees

Safe Schools
    for Everyone

Freedom to Dream

Memory Inoculation

Frozen Memories

Words of Ice

Looks of Fire

Invisible Children

Counterfeit
    Happiness

An Invisible Person

Falling Into a
    Nightmare

INTEGRATING ART AND CREATIVE WRITING INTO CORE CURRICULUM AREAS: COMBINING ART AND LITERARY THEMES THAT CAN BE APPLIED TO CORE CURRICULUM SUBJECTS

The making of art is an act of commitment to the future. The acts of drawing and writing each provide a psychomotor process that offers cathartic possibilities. Combining them in joint projects can be significantly effective. In addition to writing's capacity to discharge emotional energies, drawing affords youngsters the opportunity to reshape their pain and make something they can externalize and control. Art enables students to gain some distance from their pain and helplessness if that is their need.

Integrating these two skills into small-group projects allows students to select the medium that would best utilize their strengths, increasing their personal growth. Incorporating art and writing into core curriculum subjects permits teachers the flexibility of infusing healing activities into tight schedules and limited time slots.

Ad Campaigns

Projects for groups of three to five: create an ad campaign or promotional brochure for the following issues or events:

Save the wetland

A children's rights document and campaign

Save the wild horses

A school that is safe for all

Save the whales

Recruitment brochure for police or safety forces that focuses on meaningful opportunities to serve children, families, and communities

Promotion of gun locks

Safe storage of guns and ammunition

Guidelines for selecting honest and safe Internet chat rooms

A "menu" for feeding the mind

A community "lead-out" campaign

A "Smiley Smokeout" campaign for the community

A rite of passage

Your group's light to the world

"How to Grow Relationships With Caring and Trusted Adults"

Differences honored

A life journey roadmap

Building peaceful communities

Creating a community of hope

A home security system

Ending racial profiling

Ending housing discrimination against children

Child-friendly emergency rooms

Child-friendly visiting rooms in prisons

Child-friendly funeral homes

Heroes and role models

Building a community fit for children

Suggested topics in Chapter 6 (under "Logos") can also be adapted to creating brochures.

Comic Books

Have students, working in groups of three to five, create comic books on the themes listed below. Tell the students to expand the story line and create the endings that they desire. You, the teacher, determine the required length of the comic book based on available time.

A youngster who creates a dream machine

A youngster who builds a ladder to the stars

A youngster who finds magic glasses that empower him or her to see the world as he or she needs it to be as opposed to the way it seems

A flying bicycle that will take youngsters *only* to places where they are safe and respected by adults

A comic book about Robert Frost's statement, "Good fences make good neighbors"

A group of children who earn money to contribute to save the wild horses

A group of children who collect blankets in their neighborhood to give to the homeless

A group of youngsters who walk with first and second graders (or sit around them on the school bus) to protect them from being bullied

A group of youngsters who form a neighborhood patrol to assure that primary-school children can walk to school safely

A comic book that offers advice and safety tips to primary-school children on dealing with their fears of roaming dogs as they walk to school

A group of middle school students who convince a guidance counselor to lead them in forming support sessions one lunch period a week for primary-school students dealing with loss and grief

A comic book that funeral homes could give to youngsters grieving the loss of a loved one

A comic book about a group of friends who support a student's returning to school following cancer treatments that caused hair loss

A comic book for primary-school students, providing coping skills for dealing with divorce

A primary-school student who deals effectively with living with diabetes

A primary-school student who deals effectively with living with asthma

MANDALAS

The circle is a universal symbol of continuity and growth. Mandalas have always symbolized a safe refuge of inner security. Creating mandalas affords self-discovery and healing; they are a tool for processing and externalizing frozen emotions and hurts without actually telling. The use of imagery allows one to go deeper than words.

Externalizing inner conflicts through the symbolism expressed by mandalas can bring silent relief and renewed hope. Personal mandalas offer youngsters a safe way to express powerful emotions, thus becoming their private sanctuary.

There is no right or wrong way for students to create their mandalas. Start by handing out large predrawn circles with a small dot in the center. The dot represents *their* center.

Encourage students to select colors that they sense represent the deepest meanings of who they are: their needs, fears, hurts, joys, and hopes. The shapes or forms they use in dividing the circle are private paths to the central dot—to their selfhood.

Suggest students feel free to start over as many times as they desire until they get to the inner place they want to reach.

Allow the meanings of the colors and shapes used to remain personal, but encourage students to privately interpret or decipher what the colors and shapes mean to them. Support them in using their personal mandala as a springboard into their inner self and their inner truths.

Offer these tools for connecting with their mandala's unique meanings for them:

Imagine yourself very small; pretend you are walking inside your mandala as if it were a room.

Write down the words that come to you as you look at your completed mandala.

Give it a title that sums up your first impression.

Describe what the colors mean to you, what feelings or memories they generate.

Describe what the empty spaces represent, if there are any.

List and describe the shapes within your mandala and what they mean to you.

Write what you interpret to be the central theme.

These interpretations should remain the student's private possession, according Susanne F. Fincher (1991) in her book *Creating Mandalas.*

Here are some additional suggestions for personal mandalas that you can give your students:

Create your inner mandala and your outer mandala.

Divide the circle into four areas, to represent who you know yourself to be physically, mentally, socially, and spiritually.

Create mandalas that express your understandings of the following, and write down your descriptions or interpretations.

Truth	Dignity	Grief
Leadership	Hope	Belonging
Empathy	Respect	Impulsivity
Courage	Creativity	Trusting relationships
Personal power	Conflict resolution	Aggression
Forgiveness	Personal pain	Vulnerability
Confidence	Betrayal	Manipulation
Inner strengths	Rejection	Remorse
Relaxation	Discrimination	Despair
Justice	Loss	Power struggle
Integrity	Disrespect	

4

Social Studies and History

Creative Topics

The cathartic process of changing story endings and reversing the power status of characters by empowering the powerless offers multiple advantages in classes on history. Not only does the process promote reduction of deep stress and anxiety; it makes history come alive. These activities can make history relevant and riveting for students who may be overwhelmed by their struggles in the present.

These projects, which require research, can be approached as individual or small-group activities for independent studies or extra credit. Topic or issue choice by students is essential for meaningful symbolic connections and processing.

Encourage students to include references to the times and living conditions they learn about in their research. Including the hypothetical emotional impact of an event or situation on historical characters permits students to connect with their own internal interpretations and perceptions of helplessness, injustice, and struggles if those hidden perceptions are a part of them.

Be prepared: as students connect with hypothetical cases of struggle, they may project strong personal feelings into the scripts or stories. These strong emotions may call for fictional responses that project aggression, violence, or revenge. This is the purpose of the activity: to offer a *symbolic* projection of the student's sense of helplessness, thereby averting actual violence. If your school abides by zero-tolerance guidelines, you, the teacher, must be your students' advocate and ensure that these symbolic projections will not be misinterpreted by anyone, especially the school's administration.

Determine the length of the projects on the basis of your class schedule.

HISTORICAL CARTOONS AND STORYBOARDS

Have students, working individually or in production teams, create pictographic cartoon books or storyboards about the following hypothetical historical events or experiences:

A 14-year-old drummer in the Connecticut Militia of the Continental Army in 1779

A 15-year-old boy from New Jersey impressed into the British Navy in 1769

A 13-year-old whose parents and church congregation volunteered to support the Africans from the *Amistad* during their trial in Boston

Two youngsters who helped their parents clear their land and build a cabin and sheds on the frontier in Illinois in 1831

A 14-year-old who worked in a Pennsylvania coal mine six days a week, 10 hours a day, in 1851

Sojourner Truth and her experiences from 1843 to 1851

Clara Barton's efforts as a field nurse during the Civil War

How the Fisk Jubilee Singers from Fisk University, a Freedom School, might have created their own words to the melody "My Old Kentucky Home," by Stephen Foster, in 1871 (include the new words)

Theodore Roosevelt's childhood plagued with health problems in the 1870s

A 12-year-old immigrating to the United States with his or her family in 1873 (include what the 12-year-old would choose to bring along and why)

An 11-year-old traveling with his or her family in a wagon train from southern Illinois to a homestead on the plains in 1880

A Sioux preteen sent to an Indian School in 1882 (include how he had to turn in his tribal clothing for a uniform, get a haircut, and eat at a table for the first time; also include how he was forbidden to use his own language)

A 12-year-old girl who works 10 hours a day in a dress factory in New York City in 1896 because her mother has tuberculosis

A 10-year-old and family who arrive at Ellis Island to be processed as immigrants in 1907

Albert Einstein's school experiences in the 1890s

A 14-year-old who was afraid to go to work in 1918 and 1919 because of danger of getting influenza

A 10-year-old traveling with his or her family and dog, along with the household items they could squeeze into their old truck, as they left Oklahoma in 1935 for California

Three young friends who collect all the tin cans, aluminum, copper, rubber, and cooking grease they can find for the war effort in 1943

Sadako and her inspiring paper crane story in Japan in 1946

How Eleanor Roosevelt labored to have the United Nations develop United Nations International Children's Emergency Fund (UNICEF) in the 1950s

The story of Jonas Salk and how he developed the polio vaccine in the 1950s and why this was so important to children

Two Black youngsters traveling with their parents from a sharecropper's farm in Mississippi to industrial Detroit, Michigan, on segregated trains in the 1950s

How Neil Armstrong prepared for and became the first man to walk on the moon in the late 1960s

Ruby Bidge and her experience as the first Black to be integrated into the public schools in New Orleans, Louisiana, in the 1960s

A 13-year-old whose older brother was arrested on his college campus in 1969 for demonstrating against the Vietnam War

The child of a South Boston school crossing guard when students from the urban area were being bused to his or her elementary school in 1985 and angry protesters marched and harassed the incoming students

A homeless child and mother on the streets of the largest town near you as winter approaches in 1991

Feel free to interchange any of the subjects or topics in any of the comics, cartoons, or interview scripts.

FICTIONAL COMIC BOOKS ABOUT HISTORICAL CHARACTERS

Have students create a fictional comic book about the imaginary return of the following historical characters. Ask students: If the person you chose returned today, what would his or her impressions be? What might your person be the most thrilled about and the most sad or disappointed about?

George Washington	John Muir	Medgar Evers
Benjamin Franklin	the Wright Brothers	Jesse Owens
Frederick Douglass	Mark Twain	Jackie Robinson
Meriwether Lewis and William Clark	Woodrow Wilson	Eliot Ness
Samuel Morse	Alexander Graham Bell	Helen Keller
Oliver Wendell Holmes	Henry Thoreau	Jim Thorpe
Booker T. Washington	Rachel Carson	Sergeant Alvin York
Chief Seattle	Dwight Eisenhower	Amelia Earhart
	Richard Byrd	Marian Anderson

Feel free to interchange characters with those listed in other areas of this book.

ARTISTIC MEDIA PROJECTS FOR HISTORY OR SOCIAL STUDIES

Have students create scripts for hypothetical or actual radio and video projects that relate to core curriculum subjects.

Media projects generate enthusiastic interest from today's students; electronic media shape their world, and they yearn to participate in its allure. The primal correlation between media production and literacy skills may not be obvious to many students, but this reality can become a motivational force for reluctant writers.

Whether the scripts are videotaped or recorded is actually secondary to the cathartic process of writing and would depend on available time, resources, and equipment. Nevertheless, audiotaping or videotaping the students' projects would certainly bolster their interest and commitment and increase their sense of contributing to a meaningful, permanent work.

These projects can be done by students working individually or in production teams, depending on available time and resources.

Creating Scripts for Hypothetical Radio Interviews

Write the scripts for a radio interview program of 10 to 15 minutes about the hypothetical visit by one of the following historical characters to your school today. Include what they might find the most satisfying about your school and the most distressing.

Adam Smith	Thomas Edison	Walter Reed
Patrick Henry	Susan B. Anthony	Thurgood Marshall
John Adams	Phillis Wheatley	Martin Luther King, Jr.
Thomas Jefferson	Ralph Waldo Emerson	Malcolm X
Thomas Paine		
Abe Lincoln	George Washington Carver	J. F. Kennedy
Tecumseh		Adlai Stevenson
Henry W. Longfellow	Mary Bethune	Aaron Copland
Theodore Roosevelt	Jane Addams	Langston Hughes

Assign students to write scripts for a fictional radio interview program of 15 minutes or longer with the characters in one of the following historic events:

1621—Two youngsters who were part of the "first" Thanksgiving and chatted with several Native Americans who attended with their fathers (since this is fictional, resolve the language issue as you wish)

1730—An 11-year-old who is an apprentice to a cabinetmaker in Boston and is missing his family

1774—A 12-year-old whose grandfather was a Loyalist and whose father was an ardent Sons of Liberty volunteer (How did the youngster deal with this, and what were his or her personal feelings about the issue?)

1825—Sacagawea and her dilemma over having unwittingly helped Lewis and Clark open her homeland to settlers as the result of her yearning to find her own people (this realization might have come to her 20 years after the expedition)

1838—Two youngsters who walked with their family and relatives on the Trail of Tears from Tennessee to Oklahoma

1845—A youngster in Oberlin, Ohio, whose parents were part of the Underground Railroad and hid escaping slaves in the basement despite the dangers

1864—A newly freed slave in Georgia who cannot read or write but has to find a way to support his or her younger siblings

1864—Two young infantry soldiers during the Civil War who were cousins and who fought at Shiloh, one as a Confederate, the other as a Union soldier

1864—A 15-year-old son of a blacksmith in Georgia who evaded serving in the Confederate Army because he didn't want to fight to support the wealthy plantation owners' way of life

1864—The children of a man from New York who paid money to avoid being drafted into the Union Army while their poor neighbor had to serve because he didn't have the funds to buy his way out

1864—A 13-year-old bugler in the Civil War who witnessed death and the pain of wounded men

1865—A young freed slave who joined the Union Army and was given a rifle

1865—The mourners who came to their local railroad station to observe Abe Lincoln's funeral train

1865—Three youngsters whose family plantation and crops were totally burned and destroyed during Sherman's march to the sea

1889—A group of orphan children from New York City who are traveling by train to the Midwest to be adopted by farmers

1918—A youngster whose father has just returned from World War I after being gassed and is now blind

1920—Franklin D. Roosevelt's doctor after he has just explained to FDR's family that the president has polio

1933—An 11-year-old whose father has been without work for more than a year and now helps the father work as a street peddler in hopes of earning some money

1942—A Japanese family interned in a California War Relocation Camp

1953—The children of a civil service employee in the U.S. Department of Justice who was indicted and labeled a Communist sympathizer and lost his job, which forced the family to live in poverty and move to an inexpensive apartment in a different area of the city

1956—Rosa Parks *after* her refusal to yield her bus seat (ask about her need to work and earn money, among other things)

Writing Radio Scripts for "What If . . ." Programs

Ask students, working individually or in small groups, to write the scripts for fictional 15-minute radio programs (longer, if your schedule permits) about the following situations. Have the students create the outcomes they desire and portray the impact their outcome would have on the characters, the society, and the community.

"If" George Washington had agreed to become the king of the colonies instead of the elected leader of a democratic, representational government

"If" Aaron Burr's shot had missed Alexander Hamilton

"If" the colonial forces had lost at the Battle of Fallen Timbers

"If" Abe Lincoln had survived the assassination attempt

"If" it had been required that children of slaves be taught to read

"If" Sam Houston and Davy Crockett had won at the Alamo

"If" the Lusitania had not been sunk in 1914

"If" the U.S. Congress had ratified the League of Nations in 1919

"If" Martin Luther King, Jr., had lived 20 more years

"If" the Endangered Species Act had been passed and signed 100 years earlier

"If" the drive for women's right to vote by Elizabeth Stanton and Susan B. Anthony had been successful in the 1870s

"If" Jim Thorpe had been allowed to keep his Olympic medals

"If" Theodore Roosevelt had not provided the leadership for the federal government to establish national parks and preserves

"If" Jackie Robinson had decided not to play baseball for a major league team

"If" "Blackjack" General John Pershing had agreed to accept Blacks in the U.S. Army in World War I

"If" President Harry S. Truman had not decided to recall General Douglas MacArthur in 1948

"If" your school had water fountains for students who participated in college prep courses and separate ones for all others

Creating Public Service Announcements

Have students create 90-second public service announcements related to the following issues in social studies or health. Tape-record the announcements if possible and present them to community public health agencies or other appropriate organizations.

Qualified teens' registering and voting

Safe storage of guns and ammunition

Preteens' abstaining from smoking

Avoiding high-cholesterol foods

Ways to relieve personal pain without using drugs

Suicide prevention

Homophobia

A campaign by "Teens for Schools, Not Jails?"

Young people's uncertainty over being associated with peers of another class, race, or belief system or religion

Fears over being labeled gay or lesbian

Opposing cliques

Embracing diversity

Building a culture of peace and a sense of security

Building trust and self-respect among youth

Developing youth's leadership skills

How girls want to be treated by boys

How boys want to be treated by girls

Promoting the rights of all children

Being able to laugh at oneself

Overcoming fears of immigrants

5

Character Education

Esteemed character qualities, such as honesty, respect, and consideration, are not acquired through an intellectual process alone. Yet as educators, we are naturally inclined to rely on the act of teaching as the solution.

However, the areas of the brain involved in monitoring inappropriate behaviors and antisocial actions are not part of the central nervous system (see Chapter 2). The presentation of character flaws is not a behavioral *choice* resulting from cognitive thinking, and so we cannot simply teach children out of problematic behaviors. Students presenting unacceptable behaviors require an additional step: the opportunity to engage in a recovery process.

The best chance of changing counterproductive behavior patterns requires an understanding of the root causes. The research on the correlation between early childhood experiences and the presentation of aggression, bullying, and scapegoating has been flooding literature since the turn of the twenty-first century. Ricky Greenwald's book *Trauma and Juvenile Delinquency* (2002) is one example that focuses attention on the need for early transformative interventions.

Youngsters who have had minimal attachments, shocking losses, or terrifying experiences are not able to integrate cognitive examples of inspiring and respected social skills into their behavior patterns automatically. They first have to defuse and externalize the memory of fear and helplessness, which is the intent of this entire book. This reality does not mean the intentions of sincere educators are ill-placed or unnecessary. Students who have had the good fortune to experience nurturing, safe relationships in their young lives will be able to translate character education into strengthened prosocial skills and behaviors. For this reason, character education is a value-based core curriculum topic in many elementary and middle schools.

However, as educators, and in light of current neurological evidence, we must be realistic about our expectations for those students whose behaviors generate our deepest concerns and frustrations. These students require the additional steps of transformation activities for character education to take root.

When individuals avoid important challenges, it's not because the problems themselves are too difficult; it's because their anger, fear, and frustration make it impossible for them to trust others and themselves. The type of processing that is essential for such transformation to take place can happen only in safe environments, free from any possibility of being shamed.

Metaphorical and creative explorations advance and empower students. True character education is pure process; it is not training that is outcome oriented.

It would be helpful to recognize that the students who might benefit the most from the following activities may be the most challenging youngsters we teach. They need us not to give up on them despite their behaviors. Some of them may require additional intervention services through referrals.

INTERNAL STRENGTHS: EMOTIONAL INTELLIGENCE

The internal strengths that are so essential for safe communities and sustained democracy have become a central focus of all levels of government, the mental health system, and the field of education. When the practice of personal integrity seems to be evaporating in society, it seems improbable that schools alone can restore the moral fiber of the country.

Children's basic character is already formed when they enter kindergarten. Their ability to practice a code of values that exemplifies integrity and fairness requires that they have experienced safe, nurturing, and empathetic relationships. Caring relationships literally grow the brains that permit children, and the adults they become, to demonstrate character strengths.

Students who have not had the nurturing and security essential for the development of moral strengths can be "coached" in prosocial skills if the coaching is proffered with patience and generosity.

The capacity to problem solve and make moral choices, especially when in a state of anxiety, is not available to youngsters who have experienced shocking losses or traumas. This translates into the reality that they cannot learn alternative perspectives through a cognitive or intellectual process alone. The following activities are options for character education that can be offered as the first step of transformative activity, to be followed by the character education curriculum your school system has chosen.

Helen Keller offered this guideline: "The best and most beautiful things in the world cannot be seen or even touched. They must be felt with the heart."

A Classroom Directory of Feelings and Emotions

This activity addresses issues of boundaries, self-trust, trust of others, self-regulation, and honesty.

Ask students to name feelings. List as many feelings as possible on the board. Group and consolidate them as desired.

Provide the students with paper and ask them to draw the facial expressions that best match the feelings of their choice.

Encourage them to select colors that best depict each feeling. Colors may vary from student to student, and there are no wrong associations. Some colors may end up being used for many different feelings.

Ask the students to list behavioral actions or gestures that communicate or express each feeling under their drawings.

Bind the directory either as a classroom document or for each student individually, based on interest and time.

Make audiotapes of the vocal tones or auditory expressions that are associated with each feeling.

Have students, working in small groups, write the scripts for 60- to 90-second public service announcements validating the healthy purpose of each feeling.

Discuss the processing the students are engaged in as they carry out this project. Which feelings are deemed acceptable and wholesome? Which ones have judgmental interpretations associated with them? Which ones can be misinterpreted? Misunderstood?

Remember, youngsters who have undergone neurological alterations due to incomplete attachment or other traumatic experiences have great difficulty interpreting other people's nonverbal expressions correctly. Their survival adaptations prompt the hypervigilance and instant explosive reactions to others that create chaos in areas of reduced structure in schools, such as crowded hallways, the cafeteria, or the playground.

Increased understanding of alternative interpretations of facial expressions, voice inflections, and body language can strengthen students' ability to trust themselves, their capacity to respond rather than react, and their willingness to trust others.

A Feelings Mural: Addressing All Feelings

Feelings are often metaphorically defined in terminology of travel, landscapes, or mapping. Youngsters may have experienced being swept away, flooded, or blown away by a torrent of emotions, causing them to feel out of control and helpless. Such experiences interfere with their ability to trust their feelings and themselves as they make the tumultuous journey from childhood to adolescence.

A classroom project of creating a feelings mural, adapted from a project by Karen Bovard (2000), can be comforting and stabilizing. This activity can build skills for navigating the landscape of emotions in a nonthreatening way.

Brainstorm imaginary locations for the mural. Some examples to get you started are listed below. The names are intended to generate feelings and emotions.

Brook of bravery

Bridge of broken hearts

Covered bridge of compassion

Clouds of contentment

Causeway of courage

Cliffs of contempt

Cascades of confusion

Cave of comfort

Field of forgiveness

Forest of fright

Gully of greed

House of honesty

Hills of happiness

Lighthouse of laughter

Lagoon of loneliness

Meadow of misunderstanding

Pinnacle of pride

Paths of patience

Pleasure Park

Pits of doubt

Road of regrets

Raindrops of rejection

River of rage

Rocks of revenge

Rapids of resilience

Ridges of remorse

Streams of strength

Sea of security

Swamp of sarcasm

Spring of confidence

Stairs of stability

Shoreline of spirituality

Stumps of shame

Trail of trust

Trees of thrills and joy

Thicket of tensions

Valley of vulnerability

Walkway of worry

Waterfall of wisdom

Spread out a continuous roll of paper the length of the classroom or provide each student with a two-foot section, to be fastened to the other sections to make an extended mural after the drawings are completed. Use whatever drawing or coloring applicators are best suited to the students' abilities and grade.

Each student selects one or two mural features to incorporate into his or her section. When all drawing is completed, all students are given a small sticky note on which they draw their personal icon, known only to themselves, to be placed on the feelings mural in the spot that best represents where they are in their feelings at that moment. Once a week they are given the opportunity to change the position of their icon.

This ongoing project allows youngsters to honestly identify their emotional state and develop a sense of ease with emotional fluctuations, realizing they can cope with emotional ups and downs.

A Box of Respect: Addressing Self-Acceptance, Self-Respect, and the Ability to Respect and Empathize With Others

The ability to understand and accept what our behavior reveals about ourselves empowers us to understand the reasons for our own behavior. Some of these reasons may be a surprise, even to us.

Most of us have found ourselves doing or saying things that we do not consider our best, or even acceptable. Naturally, these memories or topics are not ones we are proud of, and consequently we are reluctant to address them. They remain as a personal learning opportunity.

Often such reactions are rooted in childhood experiences of vulnerability and helplessness. Understanding and acknowledging the fears and insecurities at the base of those reactions are essential steps toward change and the growth of character strengths. Making a box of respect helps students take these important steps. Follow these directions with your class:

Collect or have students bring in shoe boxes.

Have students decorate the outside of the boxes to represent how they want others to see them. Using symbolic colors, linear patterns, drawings, and pictures from magazines and catalogs, they can depict their personal, external image.

Similarly, have them decorate the inside of the boxes to symbolically represent their true internal identity, including traits they prefer others not see or know exist. Private mementos and representative trinkets of significant experiences or issues can be added to the boxes. Allow at least a week for this portion of the project to be completed. If at all possible, store the boxes in a locked area.

Request that students privately record in their journals their reflections on their boxes, including the similarities and differences between their external and internal images and why the differences might exist.

Assign a paper in which they outline any new insights into their existing internal strengths and how they see themselves extending or broadening those character strengths.

With everyone sitting on the floor in a circle, encourage a discussion about newfound insights and understanding from this project. The teacher's making a box and then opening this discussion can prove very reassuring to the students. Confidentiality guidelines must be clearly outlined and followed. Permit students to choose whether to take their boxes home or dispose of them unopened, with the help of the janitor.

Any of the mandala activities in Chapter 3 that address feelings can be integrated into character education.

The Iceberg Project: Addressing Issues of Respect, Empathy, and Trust

For this project, instruct your students as follows:

Remember someone you had major differences with in an earlier grade or from an earlier time in your life, someone you did not consider a friend at that time but whom you now recognize as having some qualities, strengths, and interests that you could share and find compatible.

Consider the person's characteristics that you were unable to accept or feel comfortable with. These characteristics or features can be thought of as the parts of an iceberg that are visible above the waterline.

Now think of the person's qualities you find more agreeable as being the part of an iceberg hidden under the water but in existence all along.

Draw an iceberg that clearly shows the above-water and below-water parts. Identify the personal characteristics above and below the water for the person you recalled. If you can't think of someone who fits this model, focus on someone you would like to think has desirable qualities that are unseen.

Now draw an iceberg representing your own characteristics, both above and below the waterline.

Journal about your reflections, how your insights regarding the underwater portion of the iceberg might affect your relationships and choice of friends, and what you could choose to do about those issues.

Letters to Hurts: Addressing Empathy, Compassion, Courage, Anger Issues, Forgiveness, and Generosity

Persons who are unable to take ownership of their personal hurts—the pain caused by betrayal, abandonment, rejection, and shame—will be unable to extend compassion and empathy to others. Many of the creative writing activities in the Box of Respect, also address these issues.

To move from being a victim to defusing anger, to forgiving, and to developing character strengths requires great courage and commitment. Youngsters engaged in such a healing process require empathetic support, not sympathy. Engaging in this recovery process before full adolescence increases the chance for personal growth.

Have your students write a private letter to their hurts, their broken hearts. Encourage them to create designs or motifs around the edges of their letter and to use colors and linear patterns that depict the content. Provide envelopes for every letter to be sealed into. Discuss what the students want to do with the letters; they are not to be sent to anyone and must remain confidential.

Ask students to journal on how the project has affected them and what they see themselves doing differently as a result of new insights.

Drawing a Dream: Addressing Issues of Anger, Work Ethic, Forgiveness, and Hopelessness

The capacity to vision, to dream, is essential for youngsters trying to generate and strengthen a commitment to their future in spite of feeling hopeless. For those who have experienced insecure and stressed childhoods, this commitment poses a tremendous challenge. These students are often not aware of their subconscious state of mind which creates serious barriers to their motivation and commitment.

Ask students to draw their dream for a place—a town, a school, a playground—where all children are able to feel safe, respected, and valued.

Then ask them to write a detailed account of why each feature was included and how it assured the success of the dream environment. Ask them to describe how the children who live or visit this imaginary place feel and what they are able to accomplish while there that differs from what may happen in other places.

Facing Fears: Addressing Fears, Courage, Anger, and the Ability to Overcome

Internal barriers to coping with fears, real and perceived, are the result of the adrenal and limbic system (Chapter 1) and can be overwhelming for students who have been traumatized. What they interpret as a threat generates strong, explosive survival reactions.

Courage is acting in the face of fear, but survival actions are *not* the result of intellectual or rational thoughts for those youngsters with terrorizing memories. Before they can make rational choices regarding threats and fears, they have to defuse the triggers of terror. One way to begin this process of managing fears is for students to engage in an internal activity that helps them focus on the meanings that their actions have for them so that they can find the courage to face other risks that may remain. The following activity provides this opportunity.

Conduct a classroom exploration of rites of passage; approach them historically and culturally. Include research and other activities. Why are they practiced? What constructive benefits do they generate?

Then ask students to make a list of five or more personal fears. Have them select one that they want to learn to cope with and to create an imaginary rite of passage that they think would be the most helpful and would result in their gaining the internal skills necessary to cope with it.

Tell them to include the music, sounds, colors, textures, and words for their rite that would support them in this process.

Students should include the feelings of awareness they might experience as they progress through their imaginary rite and how those feelings and attitudes change as they realize they have completed the process. How would they know inside themselves that they have successfully completed their goal? How and with whom would they celebrate that completion? They can choose to keep the description of their rite of passage or discard it.

Playground Charters: Addressing Issues of Leadership, Integrity, Conflict, Hopefulness, and Justice

Leadership is motivating and guiding people to work toward the common good with more focus and power than they would otherwise have. Good leaders inspire people to believe in themselves, according to John Graham in *It's Up to Us: The Giraffe Heroes Program* (1999). However, before youngsters can assume a leadership role, they have to symbolically move through their own sense of helplessness and hopelessness. Providing for others, especially those younger, what they did not have an opportunity to experience or receive themselves can begin this transformation process.

> Ask students to create and write down a code of ethics or charter for an imaginary club available to all the youngsters at a neighborhood playground. Ask them to address issues of respect, safety (physical and emotional), fairness, trust, health, wellness, and joy.

> Suggest they decorate the margins of their charter with symbols or icons that reinforce the meanings and intent.

WHERE ARE THE HEROES?

Issues of Emotional Honesty, Leadership, Risky Behaviors, and Choices

Every generation has heroes. Often there are great differences in who they are, how they are selected, and why. The tragic terrorist attacks on the United States on September 11, 2001, created universally acclaimed heroes from the ranks of police and firefighters, figures that not all citizens thought of as heroic before that momentous date.

Students today are influenced by the entertainment industry far more and at earlier ages than their elders were. Because of vast changes in lifestyles and available time, families may have little opportunity to discuss criteria regarding hero selection within families, making this topic one of special significance in character education. Use and adapt the following activities to help your students think about heroism, ideals, and character strength.

> Assign students to conduct interviews with their parent(s) and/or grandparent(s) about those elders' heroes, how they selected them, and why. Students should ask whether their parents and grandparents have changed their heroes over the years and why.

> Assign written reports about the interviews.

> Hold a class discussion on trends, changes between the generations, and concepts learned.

> Brainstorm with your students the characteristics necessary to be a hero. What is expected of heroes today versus when their parents or grandparents were young? Do youngsters today have needs for heroes that are different from what their elders needed?

> Have students work with partners or in small groups to write a script for a 90-second public service announcement or a radio commercial that calls for heroes for their age-group. Have them perform it for the class, and lead the class in a discussion of its views of heroism.

Honoring Strengths With a Character Wall

This project addresses issues of inclusion, acceptance, respect, and being valued. Affirmations are essential for youngsters to be able to believe in themselves and their futures. Some students receive little acknowledgment for their strengths and contributions at school or home. Some students are not afforded the opportunity to feel truly included in their classroom family. All students benefit from having their character strengths honored. Follow these steps with your students to lead them to this sense of affirmation:

Discuss students' needs and desires for feeling safe and valued in their classroom family.

During the discussion, list on the board all the personal characteristics they mention that contribute to classroom security and a sense of inclusion.

Provide each student with an 8½ × 11 inch sheet of paper and announce that it represents a brick.

Ask class members to offer their interpretation of the greatest strength each of their classmates contributes to the good of the whole. Traits can be used multiple times, but you as teacher can offer alternative semantics to assure that all the "needs" listed earlier get included.

Tell students to each select the characteristic from the board that they want on their brick.

Build a character wall with the bricks on a room wall or divider.

Discuss how the students now feel about the classroom and themselves.

The Character Board Game

Games are fun and conducive to learning. As Albert Einstein put it, "All knowledge is experience—everything else is information." Try this game to enhance students' awareness of character strengths:

Brainstorm with your students and list on the board all the character traits and abilities that contribute positively to an identity that would be described as a person of character.

Provide students with unlined sheets of paper. Have them draw a line down the middle lengthwise. Then draw five lines across, creating two rows of six equal boxes. Number them one to six in the first column and seven to 12 in the second.

Hand out 12 small (1½ × 2 inch) sticky notes to each student. Have students each select the 12 traits they sense are the most significant, or preinscribe the sticky notes with the following: Honesty, Humorous, Empathy, Leadership Skills, Trustworthy, Courageous, Forgiving, Generous, Accountable, Respectful, and Self-Disciplined; also leave one sticky note blank.

Ask the students to prioritize the traits, 1 to 12.

Discuss by asking what was listed as number one, number two, and so on. Ask what was in last place. Ask what they placed on the blank note and where they placed it.

Ask the students what they have learned.

Suggest that students take their board game home and have their parents engage in the activity.

On the following day, ask those who shared the game with family what they learned.

PHYSICAL STRENGTHS

Internal Capacities for Self-Regulation and Stress Management

Youngsters' capacity to manage both stress and their reactions to anxiety-producing experiences is determined by the neurological infrastructure that was sculpted during and by early relationships, as described in Chapter 1. Some students have had subsequent traumatic experiences that have produced increased cortisol, rendering them less able to deal with stressors. In fact, excessive cortisol can actually cause the destruction of neural cells in the hippocampus, which is the center for memory and, ultimately, stress management capability.

Although the hippocampus is part of the brain itself, it is an integral portion of the autonomic, or sensory, nervous system, not the central nervous system. Today it is described as initiating mind-body functions. The mind, or brain, and the body are integrally involved in the behaviors of stress management and reactions to anxiety.

Many educators have felt dismay over the differences in the ability of today's students to cope within the school environment. Many are not able to respond with behaviors that are traditionally labeled as character strengths and contribute to healthy choices. Disrespectful and even explosive behaviors are not uncommon, generating the frequent calls for getting back to the days when students engaged in honorable behaviors and demonstrated character ideals.

Telling stressed, anxious youngsters to relax does not automatically build the stress management skills they need. Feeling nervous and not knowing why can be profoundly confusing and alarming, especially for students with terrorizing memories. To be told they should relax and take control of their sensations, only to realize their body is not complying, builds their mistrust in their bodies and in themselves.

As one fifth-grade student blurted out to his surprised teacher, "Every time you tell me to settle down, I rev up!" while he pulled on his short hair.

Before students can strengthen their ability to relax and manage stress, they need to be provided with the tools to defuse and transform their buried memories of fear and helplessness.

Stress is a security issue, an overwhelming perception of fear that we will not be able to control what happens to us or to shape our destiny. Youngsters can apply relaxation exercises with purpose and success only *after* they have begun to resolve their traumatic memories. When we adults have expectations of students that the youngsters cannot fulfill, we only frustrate ourselves and the student—and exacerbate their stress. Hyperactivity cannot be resolved with relaxation exercises alone.

Some children who have experienced incest or sexual abuse may present very compliant behavior patterns, making it unlikely that a teacher would detect their internal confusion, especially in the lower elementary grades. As they move into prepuberty, unsettling and anxious behavior patterns may emerge. As much as the students may need relaxation training, they will *not* be able to comfortably participate in any exercises that require them to lie on the floor or a mat. Observe carefully for any signs of distress, and offer an alternative they are comfortable with.

Students who have experienced repeated terrors may not be able to allow themselves to close their eyes when you begin a relaxation program. This is a survival reaction, not a disobedient choice. Be patient with them.

Finding time within your classroom's pressure-packed schedule will probably be the most difficult aspect of initiating a relaxation program. However, once youngsters have mastered the skills, they will require very brief interludes for productive engagement. Five-minute sessions of progressive muscle relaxation or imaging reinforced by soothing music at the beginning of the day or following transitions such as recess, lunch, or classroom changes offer meaningful opportunities.

A brief relaxation exercise before taking a test can be significantly effective when this practice is consistent and ongoing (Allen & Klein, 1996). Soothing music can enhance relaxation and learning. Participants tend to unconsciously match their breathing patterns to the tempo of the music. Baroque music has been proven to enhance slower, deeper breathing. Suggestions and selections are available from the Inner Coaching organization, (920) 262-0439.

Relaxation programs can also enable students to internalize character education and make it possible for them to meet expectations and integrate new behaviors and understandings.

Leading a Relaxation Exercise:

Using a soft voice and calming body language, ask students to take a comfortable position in their seats, place both feet on the floor, and rest their hands on their thighs. Dropping their head forward seems to suit most.

Progressive Muscle Relaxation Script

While the students are sitting comfortably in their seats, recite the following:

Squeeze right hand tightly, as if squeezing a squeeze ball. Hold for three or four seconds and relax. Repeat with left hand.

Now relax and breathe out as you imagine the stress leaving your body as you breathe in warm, soothing energy.

Bend your right elbow and tighten all the muscles in that arm. Hold and relax. Repeat. Repeat with the left arm. Breathe. Repeat.

Focus on your right foot and leg; tighten your toes and leg muscles. Hold and relax. Breathe deeply. Repeat.

Encourage students to feel the tension drain away in their arms and legs, replaced by a sense of soothing warmth. Repeat this exercise with the students for several days and then extend it to other parts of the body, as follows:

Tell students to relax their shoulders and neck by pulling their shoulders up to their ears, holding tightly for three to four seconds, and relaxing, breathing deeply, and repeating.

Next, tell them to relax the face by closing their eyes tightly and clenching teeth and jaw, holding, releasing, and breathing deeply.

Next, guide them to relaxing the stomach muscles. Tell them to tighten these muscles, hold, and relax, then breathe out, exhaling all the residue of tension, then breathe in again, slowly and deeply, warming their tummy. Tell the students to send the warm, soothing breath out to their legs, feet, arms, and hands and then to repeat the process again and again to spread the relaxation deeper within.

Scripts for additional exercises can be found in *Ready, Set, Relax*, by Jeffrey Allen and Roger Klein (1996). Other ideas for supplementing and supporting the suggestions in this chapter may be found in the following works:

Ayers, R. (2001). *Studs Terkel's Working: A Teaching Guide*. New York: New Press.

Biagi, S. (1986). *Interviews That Work*. Belmont, CA: Wadsworth.

Capacchione, L. (1989). *The Creative Journal for Children: A Guide for Parents, Teachers, and Counselors*. Boston: Shambhala.

Corder, C., & Brohl, K. (1996). *It Couldn't Happen Here: Recognizing and Helping Desperate Kids*. Washington, DC: Child Welfare League of America.

Fincher, S. F. (1991). *Creating Mandalas*. Boston: Shambhala.

Goldberg, C. M. (1999). *Write Where You Are*. Minneapolis, MN: Free Spirit Publishing.

Graham, J. (1999). *It's Up to Us: The Giraffe Heroes Program*. Langley, WA: The Giraffe Project.

Stuecker, R., & Rutherford, S. (2001). *Reviving the Wonder: 76 Activities That Touch the Inner Spirit of Youth*. Champaign, IL: Research Press.

In addition, the following Internet resources are helpful:

The Giraffe Project encourages people to follow lives of courage, caring, and responsibility: http://giraffe.org/giraffe

Quest International provides tools for helping youth develop positive personal and social skills and character strengths: http://synergy.smartpages.com/quest

6

Building Resiliency Through Afterschool, Summer Camp, and Recreational Programming

Opportunities to enhance the academic resiliency of youngsters are available to schools and communities in settings beyond the classroom. The benefits of out-of-school programs addressing these issues will filter back to the schools.

AFTERSCHOOL PROGRAMS

Increasing numbers of school systems are acknowledging that insecurity and alienation are educational issues they cannot afford to ignore because stability and a sense of security are major contributing factors in the learning process and the academic achievement of students. Furthermore, schools and communities are recognizing the effects of insecurity and alienation on the behavior of youth not only in schools but in neighborhoods as well.

The timing for addressing the issue of afterschool care for students could not be more opportune now that states and the whole country are focusing more than ever on increased academic achievement. Now is the time for parents, schools, and communities to advocate strongly that funding for afterschool programs must be included in all policies of educational reform and academic improvement.

By linking afterschool programming with a district's complete academic plan, the school system can assure that the program's policies and standards are consistently upheld. The ability to reinforce basic curriculum concepts and goals with more integrated, hands-on activities becomes an added advantage. Open communication between school systems and community programs benefits everyone, especially children.

From the vantage point of stress reduction and trauma transformation, afterschool programming affords an exceptional opportunity to increase academic achievement. Although afterschool program activities are structured and intentionally designed, they are more flexible than classroom routines. Integrating movement, large muscle activities, and the arts with experiential ventures provides enriched potential latitude for psychomotor access to traumatizing memories. The relaxed schedule allows for more flexibility in processing and reaching closure on complex issues.

Along with the optional aspect of afterschool programs, at least from a legal perspective, comes a somewhat more casual expectation by parents regarding content. Although tests and report cards are not integral parts of these more relaxed programs, complete confidentiality is always an absolute requirement. Building trusting, caring relationships within the school environment may be one of the most advantageous outcomes for everyone involved: student, school, and family.

Another aspect of extended-school-day programs is the chance to deepen exploration, understanding, and implementation of new information about issues relevant to the students' lives and well-being. Freedom from achievement requirements and scores allows for more hands-on extension of concepts and deductions in ways that bring vital meaning to the learning process, especially for alienated or traumatized students. Learning can become fun and stimulating again for the potentially disconnected student.

SPECIFIC ACTIVITIES FOR AFTERSCHOOL PROGRAMS

Any of the activities presented in Chapter 5 can be adapted for afterschool programs, just as the activities in this chapter can be adapted to the classroom when time and space permit.

These activities can be done individually or in small groups.

Logos

Ask students to create logos for any of the following groups or concepts. Tell the students to create a design that incorporates their ideals for the hypothetical or real entity. Also have them write the script for presenting or "selling" their design to the director of the organization or agency, their city council, the school principal, neighborhood leaders, and so on.

A safe-neighborhood association

Your school nurse's office

A caring school

Your school counselors

A local Boys & Girls Club

A local youth center

Your school band

A children's hospital

A funeral home

Your school principal's office

Your area children's protection service

A day care center

A Head Start center

A peaceful community

A safe park

PAL (Police Athletic League)

A city recreation department

An animal shelter

A community policing center

A juvenile court

An alternative school

An ambulance service

A fire station

An ADHD (attention-deficit/ hyperactivity disorder) club

An asthma club

A diabetes club

A dyslexia club

A cancer-survivor club

An animal cemetery

Add groups or agencies that appeal to your participants or community.

If participants have created a logo for a specific agency or business, encourage them to actually present their design to that organization. Your community's weekly newspaper may be interested in featuring this community contribution by area youth.

Collaborations for Creative Projects With Younger Children: Plays, Puppets, and Masks

When young people are afforded opportunities to symbolically extend to younger children what they themselves yearned for but did not receive, they vicariously begin to heal themselves. Create collaborations between youngsters in Grades 4–8 and children in lower grades or a nearby day care center. Select from the following ideas or use several of them, in whatever order fits your needs. The plays can incorporate the younger children or be performed for them.

Have students write scripts for short plays or puppet shows on any of the following topics or events. Appropriate topics in Chapter 5 can also be used.

Lonely Lion

Lost Kitten

Slinky Dragon

Nervous Fox

Scared Leopard

Angry Alligator

Rejected Puppy

A tiger who lost his roar

A monster who couldn't stop crying

Taming a nightmare

A lamb adopted by a cow

A robin who forgot how to land

A bunny who hated carrots

A dog who wouldn't sleep in his bed and slept only on the floor

A hippo who was afraid of water

Then have the students make puppets or "feelings masks." For puppets, assemble the following materials, adding others you think are appropriate:

felt

brown bags

socks

nylon stockings

one-liter clear soft drink bottle with bottom removed to allow bottle to fit over arm or hand

yarn and scraps of fake fur

If you choose masks (to use in a play or for understanding feelings), assemble the following materials:

eye masks from party store (to use as a base)

paper plates

brown bags

nylon stockings

plastic one-gallon milk cartons

felt

outgrown infant shirts (sleeves become ears)

stocking caps (to use as a base)

sun glasses (to use as a base)

baseball caps (to use as a base)

small bubble wrap

plastic or rubber packing foam

Here are some subjects for feelings masks:

fear

disappointment

broken heart

feeling safe

loneliness

joy or happiness

frustration

hopelessness

shock

love

satisfaction

calm

discouragement

anxiety or stress

hopefulness

giggles

In addition to or as preparation for a play, encourage youngsters to wear different masks and, in discussion, explore what wearing a particular mask means to them. Ask them to talk about how outside experiences can influence the way one feels on the inside.

Designing Board Games

Designing board games is a very creative process that involves issue research, spatial visioning, and complex problem solving. Spinners can be made with, or collected from, families' outgrown or incomplete games.

Allow students to select from the following topics:

Saving endangered
   species

Saving wild horses

Preserving
   wetlands

Forest Rangers

Animal protection
   officers or patrol

Kids ending
   homelessness

Kids ending hunger

Internet police

Greasy snack patrol

Couch potato rangers

Empty-calorie busters

Rangers tracking
   wild animal
   traffickers

Kids ending animal
   abuse

Lost puppy rangers
   or rescuers

Chat room rangers

Anger patrol

Rumor busters

Fear busters

Loneliness rangers

Stress busters

Broken heart
   menders

Activity

School Conditions That Help Me Feel Safe: A tool to build awareness of every student's right and need to feel safe emotionally and physically.

This prioritizing game (see page 61) can serve as a catalyst for open communication and understanding of student safety. It can also be used by counselors to gain insights into students who may be bullying or being bullied but are reluctant to disclose the problem.

Provide participants with a copy of the paper board and the page of cards printed here. The cards will need to be cut into 12 pieces. Ask students, working individually, to arrange the cards according to their priority and write on the wild card what they want it to stand for.

Either as a group or with individual students, discuss the students' arrangement of the cards, giving special attention to students' privacy needs.

Physical and Mental Exercises

Stressed students are more likely to gain and grow from this exercise if they don't sense that adults feel they *need* to strengthen these issues. Their efforts are to be symbolic; they are nurturing or giving these strengths to someone else who needs them. The phrases below can be made into chants, poetry slams, or hip-hop dance routines created by students, individually or collectively:

to strengthen someone's inner voice

to strengthen someone's weak emotions

to strengthen someone's funny bone

to strengthen someone's anxious tummy

to untangle someone's nerves

to promote someone's heart mending

to increase someone's strength of mind

to increase someone's strength of heart

to increase someone's capacity to care

to increase someone's ability to listen and hear

to increase someone's ability to cooperate

to increase someone's capacity to be patient

to increase someone's ability to smile and laugh

to enhance someone's ability to admit being wrong

to moderate someone's competitiveness

to reduce someone's tendency to be controlling

to moderate someone's tendency to tease

ADULTS MAINTAIN SELF-CONTROL	**CORPORAL DISCIPLINE IS USED**
STUDENTS ARE OPENLY LABELED FOR BEHAVIORS	**MEDIATION IS USED FOR STUDENT CONFLICTS**
FEAR AND COERCION ARE USED TO MAINTAIN ORDER	**ABSOLUTE ASSURANCES—THREATS ARE NOT USED BY ADULTS**
STUDENT SHAMING IS USED TO MAINTAIN ORDER	**MUTUAL RESPECT BETWEEN STUDENTS AND BETWEEN STUDENTS AND STAFF**
MEDIATION FOR STUDENT-STAFF CONFLICTS IS USED	**ZERO TOLERANCE ENFORCED**
WILD CARD	**NO PUT-DOWNS ALLOWED**

School Conditions That Help Me Feel Safe

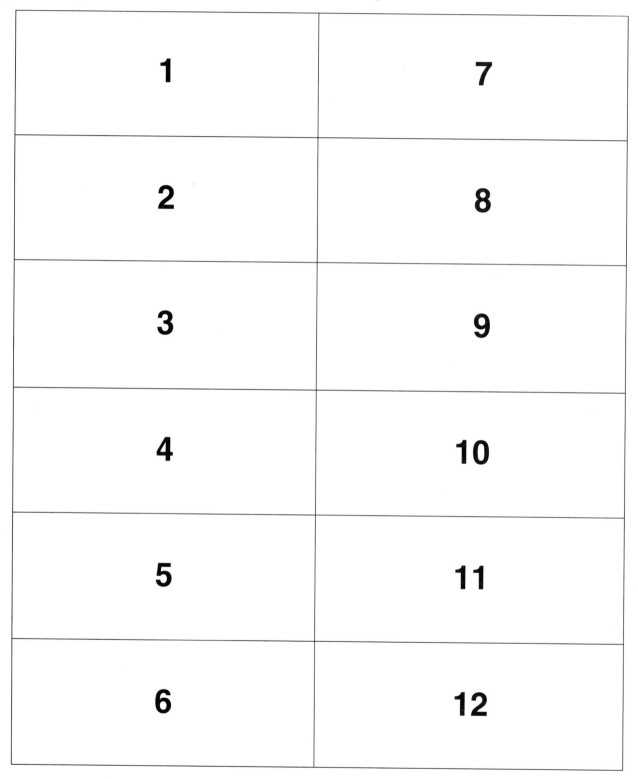

Sand Trays

Sand trays offer a very personal, introspective activity that allows youngsters to come to a deeper understanding of themselves. The activity fits very comfortably into afterschool and recreational programs and clubs. It can be a very effective tool for counselors in any of these settings.

Sand play helps children express the inexpressible and is especially helpful for those not comfortable verbalizing. The process offers youngsters a way to release feelings they may not be prepared to put into words. It allows them to be in complete control within safe boundaries as they reconstruct the "world" as they need it to be.

Sand play can be called creating an awake dream, an empowering way to solidify a child's sense of identity.

Sand tray activities require a quiet, stress-free space where time is available. Most important, the process requires a safe environment, one free from criticism but rich in empathy. Because the process is deeply personal, it demands confidentiality—nothing said or assumed goes beyond the room. If necessary, allow each student to work in private.

Materials needed: discarded shallow wooden drawers, boxes, or plastic trays, preferably 20 × 24 inches or more and three or more inches deep.

Paint the bottoms and inner sides blue to represent the sky and ponds or rivers, if desired.

Place at least two inches of clean sand in each tray.

Collect miniatures—the more the better. Ask students to take home flyers asking for miniatures the families no longer use or that are left over from holiday decorations, train setups, or aquariums. Size and scale are flexible. Garage sales and craft stores carry many items of interest. Look for the following:

Artificial branches, little trees, flowers, plants, fruits, nuts, vegetables

Stones, colored glass pieces, stars, sea shells

Toy fences, bridges, benches, lampposts

Fake butterflies and other insects; fake birds

Toy animals: farm animals (especially horses), reptiles, dinosaurs

Models of fantasy sea or land creatures, such as dragons

Model cars (including police), fire trucks, ambulances, planes, helicopters, motorcycles

Model knights, people of all sizes and ages, military, safety forces, fantasy characters

Have cardboard dividers available should someone want to do a "before and after."

Proceed as follows: Participation has to be by choice and done with as little talking as possible. Each participant is provided with a tray and encouraged to use as many miniatures as desired to create a scene. Scenes can be changed to meet their needs, even if changing them requires more than one day.

When all students have finished, invite them to share with fellow participants; allow anyone the right to pass. An attending adult can initiate the sharing by asking,

"What would you like us to know about your creation?" or "Do you like the world you built? Is it a safe place?"

Additional or alternative queries might include asking students whether their world is warm or cold, night or day, dark or bright, rainy, windy, or quiet or filled with sounds. Affirmative answers can be followed up with, for example, "What sounds?"

Discussions and issues raised have to remain confidential, with no interpretations offered by the adults or the participants.

Clubs for a Sense of Belonging and Identity

By connecting with governmental bodies or community agencies, afterschool programs can form partnerships for projects that focus on righting wrongs, a powerful process for renewing a sense of community. The opportunity to make something happen or happen better has tremendous cathartic value for at-risk or troubled youngsters. Children who have been hurt or are hurting are fascinated by issues of brokenness and fixing. For those who have experienced rejection or loss, the topic of "finding" holds special renewal and recovery meanings (Oehlberg, 1996).

Here are some examples of afterschool clubs or programs for students to help organize and become involved in:

Fix-It Toy Club—for neighborhood or church child care centers

Toy Factory—for creating and building new toys for child care centers, hospitals, and children in foster care

Doll Hospital—for fixing broken dolls or torn teddy bears for neighborhood, church, or community agencies

Games and Things—for creating new board games for children in hospitals or other care situations. Some possible board game topics: staying safe, escaping, magic gardens, anger management, conflict management, finding lost pets or lost toys

Computer Games Club—through partnership with local business or corporation; for creating computer games for their afterschool program or agency

Junior ER Club—for creating or collecting toys for children who wait in an emergency room, designing and painting a mural for a local emergency room, or making get-well cards for sick or injured children

Junior Veterinary Club—in partnership with local animal hospital or shelter; for designing and producing get-well cards for dogs, cats, and other pets; making toys for dogs or cats to take home; creating songs, rap, or stories about keeping pets safe

Junior Firefighters' Club—through partnership with neighborhood fire station; for creating and making storybooks for firefighters' children who worry about their parents' safety; making toys or books for children who have lost theirs in house fires; and creating rap, songs, or commercials about fire safety

Junior Police Officers' Club—through partnership with a community ministation or precinct station; for creating and making storybooks for children of police who worry about their parent's safety; creating rap, songs, or commercials about staying safe on playgrounds, on sidewalks, and in shopping centers; and creating board games about treasure hunts or finding lost toys or jewelry

Photography Club—in partnership with a local professional photographer, business, or corporation for supplies; for shooting photos of the ugly and the beautiful in the world around them, to be printed through arrangement with a local daily or weekly newspaper (a student journalism club could provide the story) and displayed through arrangement with municipal buildings

Journalism Club—for preparing articles on local and national compassionate and heroic acts by children and youth, youngsters who have righted a wrong, and students living in areas that have experienced a natural disaster

Local History Clubs—for interviewing elderly residents and making living history with tapes or written documents and presenting them to the public library or area historical society

Social Action Clubs—for providing opportunities that can lead youngsters toward realizing their real power to initiate attitude and policy changes regarding social justice advocacy

Adults are profoundly affected and inspired by justice campaigns led by the compassion of young people. One empowering project, titled "One Million Postcards," organized by two young sisters as an advocacy project that began with local signs and flyers and ultimately extended across the nation through the Internet, operated during the 1990s and can be applied to any issue. A short, informative video about the project is available for $10.00 from

American Friends Service Committee
1501 Cherry Street
Philadelphia, PA 19102
Phone: (215) 241-7170
Fax: (215) 241-7177

Another campaign is Free the Children USA. This project is based on the gallant efforts of Craig Kielburger (1998) to end child laborers in sweatshops.

Free the Children USA
12 East 48th Street
New York, NY 10017
E-mail: freechild@c/o.com
Web site: www.freethechildren.org

The following organizations may also provide resources for social action clubs:

Food Works
Common Roots Press
64 Main Street
Montpelier, VT 05602
Phone: (800) 310-1515

American Horticultural Therapy Association
Denver Botanic Gardens
909 York Street
Denver, CO 80206-3799
Phone: (800) 634-1603

The National Gardening Association
180 Flynn Avenue
Burlington, VT 05401
Phone: (800) 538-7476
(Request a free copy of "Growing Ideas.")

Circus Club—for providing the opportunity to build self-confidence and trust of their own minds and bodies. A circus club allows youngsters to develop and take pride in individual talents and strengths. Young people's development of empathy, along with their commitment to inquiry and learning, can be ignited by opportunities to directly and personally sense that they have something of value to offer and that they can make a difference in their community. As noted earlier, traumatic memories are body memories and can be accessed only through psychomotor activities—activities that engage the body or hands in movement. Afterschool programs afford inspiring opportunities to engage students in noncontact physical activities that can access traumatic memories in a way that provides mastery over them. These activities, which may not fit into regular academic or physical education formats, can give youngsters a way to deepen their ability to trust their own bodies by developing alternative neural pathways. Ultimately this process enhances the students' cognitive or academic capabilities.

Therapeutic physical activities that can be developed in a circus club include the following:

Magic tricks

Juggling

Gymnastic and circus acts

Unicycling

Martial arts

Ethnic and interpretive dance

Drumming—African, Pacific, and Indigenous American

Synchronized rope jumping

Information about a successful club may be requested from the following address:

The Benjamin Franklin Circus Club
Benjamin Franklin Elementary School
1905 Spring Road
Cleveland, OH 44109

These suggestions and examples are offered at many creative afterschool programs, perhaps without an awareness of why they may be meaningful to the young participants. My goal in including them is to offer insights into how they can be designed to provide the recovery opportunities that can benefit the stressed, alienated students in your community.

Crossword Puzzles

This activity allows youngsters to gain information and insights in a totally personal, private, and introspective manner. It needs to be voluntary and confidential and offered with an empathetic adult available if needed.

These puzzles are not offered as a word or language challenge. They are intended to be a tool for developing new understandings that may lead to personal release, healing, and empowerment. Encourage students to check the answer sheet when they need clues in order to proceed.

The puzzles are printed in Resource A at the end of this book, and the answers in Resource B. You may photocopy them as needed.

THEATER AND ARTS GROUPS OR CAMPS

The symbolism inherent in all art forms is the elixir that brings to traumatized children and youth the opportunity to dream and hope, to engage the wisdom of the soul.

Children need to dream a future for themselves before they can embrace one. Artistic expression has the vital capacity to heal the soul and regenerate hope and a vital sense of future. Engaging in the dramatic arts is soul work.

The opportunity to establish safe relationships with trusted adults is another significant benefit of theater groups, whether they are community based or provided through a specific service agency. Domestic-violence and youth shelters that have incorporated such projects have found them exceptionally meaningful for the presenting participants. In addition to the personal cathartic value of dramatic art presentations, they afford young people an opportunity to give important information to others and to make a difference for others.

Drama Scripts for Stage or Radio: Building a World Fit for Children

Assist students in writing scripts for a live radio program about a future in which institutions, adults, and agencies live up to the expectations and needs of children or young people. Money is not a consideration in this vision of the future.

Then allow students to practice and perform the "live" radio show, creating all the sound effects essential for telling the story and making it sound real. Record it on tape. Some possible topics include the following:

Sports or recreation programs

Housing possibilities and availability

Schools and education

Relationships and families

Foster care and juvenile courts

Conservation and ecology

Diversity and unity; issues of classism, racism, and so on

Health and health care accessibility

Safety and security everywhere; peace

Comedy Scripts

Humor, even dark humor, offers young people an opportunity to get some distance from their fears and pain. It allows them to turn something scary, ugly, and troubling into a farce that has lost its sting. The comedic value must come out of surprising twists and turns; it must not become revenge. Guide and mentor students by demanding creativity, not by making judgments.

Let students write a short script for a comedic play, movie, or stand-up comedy routine that focuses on the following fictitious characters, events, or experiences:

Dieting	Removing tattoos
Saving pets	Piercings
Stress or stress management	Couch potatoes
Emergency rooms	School dress codes
Being the middle child	Backpacks
Being hospitalized	Anger management
Dog packs	Gym locker rooms
Sibling rivalry	Gangs
Police dogs	Bullying
Riding on a school bus	Living in two houses: Mom's and Dad's
Eating in the school cafeteria	
Foster care	Sharing a bedroom with a sibling
If I made the rules	
Tattoos	Gym classes

Movement and Dance

Traumatic memories are body memories recorded in the sensory or autonomic nervous system. For this reason rhythmical body movements can bring relief and renewal.

There is no right or wrong way to express feelings through movement. Each youngster engages in a personal form of expression. Youngsters tend to be very free in using their bodies in their presentation of emotions and may not require prodding, but the activity would be more meaningful if offered as a choice rather than as a requirement.

Drumming is a very enticing accompaniment. Tape and CD recordings of African and Native American drumming are readily available.

You can suggest emotions to be portrayed or allow the youngsters to keep their inspirations private. Discussing the experience can add to the clarity of the experience but must be voluntary.

Possible themes for movement or dance are listed below:

Discovery	Excitement	Anger and rage
Fulfillment	Rejection	Fear
Relief	Loneliness	Intimidation
Resolution	Abandonment	Terror
Joy	Despair	Being at peace

Several excellent resources for therapeutic drama and dance are listed below:

- Diallo, Y., & Hall, M. (1989). *The Healing Drum*. Rochester, VT: Destiny Books.
- *Peace in the House* is a project that uses dramatic arts to raise the issues of violence and violence prevention while it trains young people in prevention strategies. For more information, contact

  > Peace in the House
  > Blues City Cultural Center
  > P.O. Box 140059
  > Memphis, TN 38114
  > Phone: (901) 323-6992
  > Fax: (901) 327-7060

- *Kenyetta Dance Theater* includes drumming and movement. To request information, e-mail kenyettaco.aol.com.

The Power of the Beat: The Rhythm of Healing

Setting rhyming words to a syncopated beat sets into motion a cathartic process that seems to truly touch the souls of youth. Young people achieve a dynamic sense of internal relief and freedom through repetitious sounds or words set to a cadence. This form of creativity integrates music and rhythm with words and poetry to generate deep, personal connections and relief. As students go with the beat, they literally peel away the layers.

Guide the youngsters to an awareness of the importance of silence as an integral part of the rhythm; encourage them to seek a balance between silence and sound.

Encourage the inclusion of additional acoustics created by the hands, feet, or mouth, plus vocals of peers as background support during readings or presentations. The goal is the externalization and transformation of buried word associations in an acceptable youth-culture process. Make audiotapes of the finished creations and consider an open-mike event for a program or camp closing.

The following word sets can serve as a beginning; encourage youngsters to add their own.

harassed, detached, bypassed

tension, detention, suspension, intervention

sass talk, trash talk, stash talk, cash talk

conformity, superiority, authority

vulnerable, unpredictable, miserable

instigated, targeted, alienated

seclusive, abusive, reclusive

intuition, distinction, humiliation, isolation

naming, blaming, shaming

trusting, busting, disgusting

discrimination, intimidation, humiliation

flaunting, moping, coping

cuff, rough, tough

assurity, security, community

picking, dissing, kicking

predictable, sustainable, enjoyable

stranded, abandoned, demanded

categorized, marginalized, alienized

fantasize, analyze, supervise

bravado, macho, commando

delayed, portrayed, betrayed

uneven enforcement, peer condonement, negative development

serious, delirious, oblivious, injurious

zero tolerance, problem tolerance, intolerance, justice solvence

observance, tolerance, consequence

troubled, overindulged, enabled, labeled, tabled

stress, distress, helplessness

strung out, hung out, kicked out

druggers, muggers, sluggers

respected, selected, invested

violence, silence, absence

compromised, objectified, classified, marginalized

altercations, tensions, detentions, suspensions, interventions

diversity, anxiety, decency

hazing, invoking, evoking, provoking, scapegoating

substance use, substance abuse, substance refuse

desiring, aspiring, solidifying, qualifying

cool, tool, fool

tap, bat, cap, rap

elitist, cliques, conflicts, rejects, super sets

hyper tense, super intense, violence, consequence

loneliness, sadness, sacredness, progress

sympathize, intellectualize, rationalize, normalize

vigilant, confidant, instant, independent

violators, perpetrators, trust projectors, hope defectors

put down, hold down, lock down, shut down

slum, numb, dumb, scum

racism, cynicism, adultism, escapism, elitism

Media Production

Activities that focus on the communication skills that form the basis of all forms of media can provide youth with a voice that is an integral part of full, responsible citizenship.

The foundation of all media and journalistic efforts is the ability to creatively use words to inspire, to empower, and to tell a story. These are also the tools for transformation and recovery. Providing young people with an opportunity to proactively explore and address societal issues is precisely the empowerment essential for self-motivation.

The symbolism that is so integral to prose, poetry, and creative storytelling affords traumatized and alienated youth the personal tools for memory transformation. This renewing process can take place without anyone's being aware it is happening, including the creator and the youth leader.

The remaining essential element in this reempowerment process is to provide young people with the privilege of being heard. Community youth organizations can perform this role.

An excellent example of a community program empowering youth in this way is PRYME (Partnership for Regional Youth Media Empowerment).

PRYME offers the following activities:

The Write Way, a creative writing and publishing program for inner-city middle school students; publishes three newsletters a year with prose and poetry from students working in neighborhood bureaus.

What Youth Think Today, a radio and television production program for high school students; a production team of 10 to 12 aspiring broadcasters produces its own half-hour radio show, aired once a week by a local station, and also does some contracted video productions.

PRYME–Net, a program in which inner-city teens learn to use computers and the Internet to produce their own interactive Web site that serves teens.

For more information on PRYME programs, contact

Dave Howell, Director, DavidH3748@aol.com
Creative Partnerships for Prevention
c/o Department of Education, Safe and Drug Free Prevention
600 Independence Avenue, S.W.
604 Portals
Washington, DC 20202-6123
Phone: (202) 260-6123
www.cpprv.org; www.prymetime.com

SUMMER CAMPS OR ACTIVITY PROGRAMS

Recreational programming through the collective efforts of schools, social service agencies, and the faith community can provide youngsters the safety net so essential for the quality of life desired by us all. Staff training in trauma and trauma transformation would be recommended, not because of the probability of serving troubled youngsters, but because of natural and fitting opportunities to make a difference. As working parents attempt to cope with ever greater stressors of fragmented time and energy, the need for community support becomes more and more imperative.

Summer overnight and day camp programs offer natural opportunities to address the more intense needs of stressed, disconnected youngsters in a spontaneous way. Some camps are designed and advertised to address issues of loss and grief or health or physical challenges. Some are designed to focus on the experiences and needs of urban, foster, or adopted children. Some are organized around a particular art form or sport.

Whatever the format or specified outreach purpose of a summer camp, they all share one strength: the opportunity to develop meaningful relationships within a structured, safe, and neutral environment. The chance to form relationships between children or youth from a variety of settings and with a variety of experiences provides a unique framework for addressing personal identity issues within an objective context. But the most substantial asset of summer camps often is the opportunity to build trusting, safe relationships between children and adults.

Since the primary requirement for empowering a youngster to transform and integrate an experience of loss or helplessness is a trusting relationship, summer camps can play a profound role in restoring hope to stressed children. Camp sponsors and leaders have this added opportunity to make a difference in the lives of many children by building on the information and references in this book. Transformation and reempowerment remain the work of the child, but camp leaders and counselors can provide the tools, the safe environment, and the support for sustaining the process. This intentional choice will need to be bolstered by staff training and support sessions.

Summer activity programs often have the flexibility and mobility to interact more directly with local or regional resources. Visiting local historical sites and cultural organizations to broaden students' understanding of personal identity issues, as well as addressing topics of social justice, can stimulate and challenge awareness and insights. These experiences can serve as the backdrop for cathartic expression, through the dramatic arts, addressing issues of loss, rejection, oppression, and maltreatment.

The summer camp for healing, organized through community collaboration for the students directly impacted by the Jonesboro Middle School tragedy in Arkansas, is an example.

With the expertise of a music therapist, a storyteller, an artist, a teacher, a trauma specialist, and others, the camp offered not only a lot of fun but variety of self-expression opportunities in a journey toward healing. For more information, contact

The Reverend David Gill
1720 Ferncliff Road
Little Rock, AR 72223
Phone: (501) 821-3063

The symbolic overlapping of issues of race, gender, and class and the hurts or wounds these issues can generate can be extensive. These hurts can be personal, cumulative, and collective, ultimately extending to entire population groups. The opportunity to address one issue can carry over to others; healing is holistic. The creative and dramatic arts afford youngsters a tangible way to give form to feelings and emotions, increasing their ability to manage those feelings proactively. The freedom achieved through this transformation process can permit young people to formulate a new perspective on their futures and perhaps even on their pasts.

One example of a summer program achieving extraordinary success is the Young African American Women teen program, whose mission is to provide girls ages 13 to 18 with counseling and artistic experiences such as dance, theater, and music. In a recent project, each girl made and painted a papier-mâché mask. For more information, contact

Rap Art Center
1941 S. Taylor Road
Cleveland Heights, OH 44118
Phone: (216) 932-9497

BOYS AND GIRLS CLUBS, SCOUTING, AND 4-H

The opportunity to dissipate hopelessness and build coping skills into lasting resiliency fits naturally into the structure of any organization for young people. National program organizations like Boys and Girls Clubs, Boy Scouts, Girl Scouts, and 4-H, for example, all have prescribed programming guidelines and frameworks that can accommodate the causal defusing of traumatic memories. What is lacking is appropriate awareness and training for project leaders and volunteer leaders.

The natural fit between specific social topics and various badge or patch requirements has yet to be developed. Active advocacy is needed to incorporate intentional transformation activities in these organizations. The voices of volunteers and parents supporting such activities could make a tremendous difference.

The goals of programming for youngsters within any of these organizations are virtually the same: to build self-confidence and leadership through empowerment and skill development. Often a more direct outcome goal is to avert victimization as well as aggression and violence. These goals are the same as those of this volume and everything cited within it.

Youngsters join counterculture gangs for very real and urgent reasons. Gangs become a culture unto themselves and a substitute for what young people need developmentally but do not find. Our best opportunity for preventing youth from joining detrimental gangs is to offer groups that meet *all* their needs, social, emotional, physical, and intellectual, in addition to spiritual.

All the youngsters who participate in afterschool or community programs attend a school of some sort. Creative activities for symbolic transformation of the helplessness of trauma will not, by themselves, permit all stressed and anxious students to learn and achieve to their full potential. If students sense that the school climate cannot ensure emotional as well as physical security, they cannot focus on academics.

School climates that permit students to feel safe and secure will significantly build the academic achievement of chronically stressed and anxious youngsters. Student school experiences beyond the classroom are the topic of the rest of this book.

Part III

Schools That Work

A Sense of Safety for All

7

Sustaining
Enhanced Learning
Environments

Across America, at the very time our nation is achieving technological advancements and medical breakthroughs, issues of schools and education have become a national concern. The academic achievement of the majority of our students is faltering, much to the dismay of educational, business, and government leaders and, most important, of the students themselves.

The first nationwide report card for fourth and eighth graders was released in the fall of 2003 by the National Assessment of Educational Progress. Although the scores had improved compared with previous years, state by state only 31 percent of America's fourth graders read at or above grade level. Certainly the issue of academic improvement has not been fully resolved.

Building meaningful relationships with students has not been a component of most teacher training. Many dedicated educators feel that investing energy in relationships with the emotionally needy students in their classrooms could totally drain them and speed up burnout. The news that students need relationships with authentic, caring adults may not sit comfortably with a middle school teacher facing well over 100 preadolescents every day.

The 1997 National Longitudinal Study of Adolescent Health survey concluded that feeling connected to their teachers is the most important educational factor influencing teens to avoid counterproductive behaviors. Rebuilding trust in themselves and their school community will come only through relationships between students and their teachers. Trusting relationships are essential for motivating the academic achievement essential for productive citizenship.

OPPORTUNITIES FOR CLASSROOM CHANGE

Avoiding the Stress of Threats

Through the research cited in earlier chapters, we have come to understand how neurological adaptations to loss and trauma cause children and youth to respond to security threats, real and perceived, with automatic fight-or-flight reactions. How might this knowledge, coupled with the awareness of the counterproductive nature of threats, be integrated into attempts to resolve the issues of school safety and diminished academic achievement?

For example, let's consider how acutely anxious children cannot access their cortex while sensing a potential or perceived insecurity or threat. Now place that student in a fourth-grade class about to take a proficiency test. Many students can cope with that challenge, but acutely anxious children perceive it to be a threat, not a purposeful challenge. The anxiety means these students, regardless of IQ, the quality of teaching, or the amount of preparation, will not be able to access their cortex to retrieve what has been successfully processed and learned. The outcome can be disappointing—and it is avoidable.

Testing used to be a means to an end, a process for determining which teaching strategy was most productive. Unfortunately, proficiency tests today all too often become an end in themselves and thus an end to the self-confidence of the student and the teacher. In some cases proficiency tests mean an end to a student's participation in any further form of education.

The correlation between the use of threats in classroom management and learning achievement is another issue for reexamination in light of neurological research. Consider the classroom where the teacher threatens that if there are any more disruptions, the troublemakers will be sent to the office. In that classroom every student, and particularly the anxious ones, will sense the instructor is incapable of taking personal initiatives to ensure steadfast predictability and security. Tensions and anxieties escalate. With adrenaline surging, the students with internalized panic and fear experience another wave of stress—and reduced cortical processing. Another opportunity for learning has been lost.

Students with anxieties do test their teachers, but not to see what they can get away with. They are testing to see if their teacher can deal with the students' fears, which are misinterpreted by adults as anger.

When anxious students sense the adult cannot cope with the youngsters' "anger," their anxiety rises.

Anxious students perceive immediately when an adult in their presence has lost self-control. Many children have learned from personal experience that their vulnerability increases when adults are not in control of themselves. Stressed students equate classroom stability with personal security. Teachers who are unable to remain centered and who play into students' anxiety by issuing threats create environments that trigger acting-out behaviors and reduced cortical learning.

Alternative Responses

Responding to acting-out behaviors by addressing the unmet needs or causes, as opposed to escalating the students' symptoms, would allow schools to reduce aggressive actions and increase academic achievement while maintaining the bonds of community.

A schoolwide focus, in kindergarten and the primary grades, on restoring academic resiliency could provide a head start on reducing acting-out behaviors in Grades 4–8. Primary students are inherently responsive to healing activities, as outlined in *Making It Better* (Oehlberg, 1996). Establishing a schoolwide culture of respecting the need of stressed students to feel safe from emotional, psychological, and physical threats will greatly enhance overall achievement.

The accompanying table presents a framework to help teachers understand possible causes of problem behavior, enabling them to choose alternative responses.

Underlying Issues	Cumulative Unmet Needs or Causes	Behavioral Tendencies or Symptoms
Fears, terrors	Need to feel safe and secure	Oppositional
Lack of personal safety	Need to feel attached	Belligerent
Lack of trust	Unresolved losses	Impulsive
Revenge for traumas	Need to feel respected	Aggressively raging
Guilt, regrets (for not intervening or stopping an injury or fatality)	Need to feel valued	Disrespectful
Powerlessness	Need to trust self	Argumentative
Rejections	Need for empowerment	Harassing
Marginalization	Need for self-confidence	Teasing
Lack of personal confidence	Need for intrinsic powers	Sullen
Arrested empathy	Need for social skills	Joyless
Shame and self-hate	Need for coping skills	Cynical
Hopelessness	Need for spirituality Need for hope	Passive
Futurelessness	Need to sense a future	Unmotivated

CLASSROOM GUIDELINES

Stressed students equate being controlled with being vulnerable, and yet they absolutely require a predictable sense of security in order to be active learners. How can a classroom management style assure security without being interpreted as a potential threat by students operating out of an internal sense of helplessness? The essential strategy for maintaining environments conducive to learning is for teachers to offer choices within set limits.

Inviting students to participate in setting classroom rules that will permit *everyone* to feel safe can meet these seemingly contradictory requirements. The reference to "everyone" includes teachers, and "choices" means only the options you, the teacher, can allow within the framework of sustained security and learning.

When students determine the rules, they are far more inclined to follow them.

It would be very natural for dedicated teachers to experience frustration over the behavioral disruptions that quite consistently interfere with the concentration of the more motivated students. However, contracts today hold teachers accountable for the achievement of *every* student in each classroom.

Restorative Discipline

Creating environments where emotional security, trust, *and* learning flourish is emerging as one of the most beneficial approaches for building resiliency in schools and students (Henderson & Benard, 2000). Restorative, or holistic, discipline offers a viable alternative to the use of threats and the punitive discipline of rejection.

The term "discipline" is a derivative of the word "disciple" and means "teach." To many, many students, however, it has come to mean "punish," "separate," or "reject."

Youngsters with insecure attachments, and the neurological imprint that creates, cannot cope with the possibility of additional rejection. To those students, who are most likely to be presenting acting-out behaviors, the rejection inherent in a disciplinary threat exacerbates their sense of insecurity and anxiety, and learning shuts down.

Restorative discipline enhances trust and security, conditions essential for active learning.

"Discipline That Restores"

"Discipline That Restores" focuses primarily on restoring students' trust in themselves, their school, and in others. It's about returning a student's sense of self-growth and security. Misbehavior is viewed primarily as an offense against human relationships and secondarily as a violation of school rules (which are written to protect safety and fairness in human relationships).

The primary victim of the misbehavior is the one most impacted by the offense. The secondary victims are others impacted by the misbehavior and might include students, teachers, parents, administration, and community.

Discipline That Restores (DTR) is a process to "make things as right as possible" (Claassen, 1993).

> Restorative discipline considers inappropriate behaviors primarily as a relationship issue, and secondarily as a violation of a school rule.
>
> The primary victim of the offense is the one most impacted, and secondary victims—other students and adults—play a role in building resolutions and a sense of security.
>
> The goal of discipline that restores is to rebuild a sense of security, both physical and emotional, for all involved.
>
> Restorative discipline considers both the danger and opportunity afforded by inappropriate behaviors and conflicts. It recognizes that anger is actually fear, and provides an opportunity to rebuild a sense of security.
>
> Restorative discipline advocates intervening at the earliest point and recognizes that all discipline results in restoring everyone's self-regulation.
>
> Discipline that restores focuses on building a resolution through the participation of all those in conflict.

Discipline that restores recognizes that not all participants can choose to cooperate until they perceive emotional security. This requires that they fully understand the goal is to build a resolution that allows all involved to feel safe. It also requires that all participants understand and acknowledge the consequences of their decisions, both positive and negative.

Restorative discipline requires that all participants are essential for building resolutions by acknowledging the needs of all. Every person involved has to verbally commit to his or her portion of the solution.

Restorative discipline requires follow up since keeping agreements is key to building a trusting community.

DTR provides teachers a productive classroom strategy for controlling the learning environment, not the students. It basically incorporates the concepts of Dr. Becky Bailey, described in Chapter 1. For more information on DTR, visit www.discipline thatrestores.org.

Stress Reduction Strategies for the Classroom

Strategies for personal or individual stress management were discussed in Chapter 2. Stress reduction for classroom environments, even an entire school, can enhance achievement levels and bring greater professional fulfillment for educators.

You, the teacher or staff member, have the greatest role in creating a classroom environment of security and stress reduction. All of your students, especially those with anxieties and perceptions of helplessness, are devoted to detecting your non-verbal cues that indicate your stress level. These students have interpreted your equilibrium status within the first minutes of class time, based on your breathing patterns and your voice pitch and volume.

High stress levels tighten one's diaphragm, hindering deep breathing. Sensitivity to discerning short, shallow breaths and elevated voice pitch is an automatic part of anxious students' hypersensitivity. When attending adults are not in complete control of themselves, students' sense of vulnerability is triggered, and their anxiety escalates, referred to by Becky Bailey as "getting hooked" (discussed in Chapter 2).

Our ability as educators to sustain learning environments of minimal stress will depend on how we have resolved any of our own childhood memories of helplessness and anxiety. If we have not been afforded the opportunity to complete such transformations, the healing activities offered in this resource could serve as key exercises for us as well as for students.

Teacher Transition Times

During morning commutes between home and school, fully optimize the transition time with soothing music and breathing exercises. To continue the practice on return trips would extend the benefits.

Beginning of the Day and All Other Transition Times for Students

Briefly reduce lighting levels.

Connect with each student as each one enters the room.

Play soothing music as a soft background during opening moments and announcements. Specialized music for relaxation is available from Calm Kids at www.calmkids.com@aol.com.

Use rituals and predictable routines.

Use and maintain a low voice pitch and volume; gain attention by flicking lights or other nonescalating practices.

Engage students in a brief relaxation and breathing exercise.

Engage students in the transforming activities described in previous chapters.

Eliminate threats and shaming.

Be sensitive to students' needs to save face.

Use humor.

Identify problems, not blame.

Engage students as problem solvers.

Focus on safety as the rationale for guidelines, limits, and teacher interventions.

State clearly that your primary role as teacher is to ensure safety for everyone, including yourself.

Consider incorporating therapy dogs into particularly unsettled classes. To learn of available therapy dogs and handlers in your area, contact Therapy Dogs International; phone: (973) 252-9800; e-mail: tdi@gti.net; URL: www.tdi.dog.org.

Total-school stress reduction is essential and is discussed in Chapter 8, on school safety.

Here are further resources for stress reduction:

The Good Grief Program—provides training and consultation to educators and child care workers before a loss occurs so they are prepared to assist children and adolescents in crisis.

Boston Medical Center
One Boston Medical Center Place, Mat 5
Boston, MA 02118
Phone: (617) 534-4005
Fax: (740) 534-7915

I Feel Better Now—group intervention for 6- to 12-year-olds; includes student worksheets, leader's manual, and support materials.

Institute for Trauma and Loss in Children
900 Cook Road
Gross Pointe Woods, MI 48236
Phone: (313) 885-0390
Fax: (313) 885-1861

The Healing Arts Project—offers new creative-arts assessment and therapeutic information for maltreated children.

CIVITAS
Child Trauma Programs
Baylor College of Medicine
Department of Psychiatry
www.civitas.org (caregiver section)

School-Based Mourning Project, in collaboration with the Northwest Family Center of DC Commission on Mental Health—provides group mourning support and processing for multiple losses, traumas, and deprivations associated with urban living.

Bruce Sklarew
5480 Wisconsin Avenue, Suite 211
Chevy Chase, MD 20815
Phone: (301) 652-0889

The Safe Harbor Project, a Victim Services Program—offers a comprehensive school-based victim assistance and violence prevention program designed to help students, faculty, and families cope with violence at school, at home, and on the streets.

Victim Services
2 Lafayette Street
New York, NY 10007
Phone: (212) 577-7700

8

School Safety Issues

Violence Prevention

GENERATING A UNITED EFFORT:
LEADERSHIP AND STAFF DEVELOPMENT

Today's teachers need support and resources to increase the skills necessary to reach and teach the most stressed and anxious students. One-size teaching will not generate the academic achievement required of schools by the No Child Left Behind Act. Educational leadership that does not take into account our current understanding of neurological development and how it affects the way youngsters learn will have minimal success in reaching the achievement goals demanded of schools in the next decade.

In 1996 the Council of Chief State School Officers adopted standards for school leaders. The first standard suggests that an educational leader is one who promotes the success of all students by facilitating the development, articulation, implementation, and stewardship of a vision of learning. However, the process of learning is not a formula of abstract, mechanical methodology; it is molded by the way a youngster's brain has been hardwired and shaped by very early relationships and experiences. In the twenty-first century, educational leaders need the knowledge acquired through cross-disciplinary research.

The translation of neurobiological research into educational strategies is slow, however. Education and social science journals have extensively defined and described the problems with today's students, teachers, and schools. School reform is a popular topic, but the majority of the prescribed solutions constitute reconfigurations of what has been done before, what used to work, or what should bring success. The resulting stress and frustration for students and educators continue to mount as state achievement criteria rise (Meier, Kohn, Darling-Hammond, Sizer, and Wood, 2004).

It would seem obvious that more of the same is not moving us closer to the genuinely desired outcomes.

Over the past 20 years, the education of America's children has become politicized. The capacity of schools to create and maintain a sense of community through mutually respectful relationships fell out of balance with the overwhelming focus on competitive academic achievement. Consequently, meeting the emotional needs of students was divorced from educational environments at the precise onset of "childhood changed," that is, the very time when children's sense of connectedness with communities and time-stretched families has diminished.

Somehow during this time of scrutinizing public education, parents and schools will have to settle on a balance that enhances learning while supporting the emotional and spiritual development of all students. Do we need better schools or schools that can better meet the total needs of students?

Integrating the neurological information of this book requires leaders who are willing to examine and shift their assumptions, beliefs, and practices. Educational strategies that worked adequately for children of previous generations will not successfully reach and teach the more stressed students sitting in today's classrooms. Implementation of the educational shifts implied by current neurological research will require intense top-to-bottom motivation and support. The ways anxious students learn require changes in teaching styles that are so broad and deep that few teachers will embrace them without continuous encouragement from their school leaders. Student learning remains the fundamental purpose of schools, and professional development is an integral part of school improvement.

The Standards for School Leaders, formulated by the Council of Chief State School Officers as a shared vision of education, define the leadership role as ensuring the management of the organization, operations, and resources for a safe, efficient, and effective learning environment. Appreciating the needs of today's learners for emotionally and psychologically safe schools presents the greatest challenge for administrators and teachers.

The best curriculums available will not promote deeper learning if the issue of emotional security—as defined by students, not adults—is not understood. When a classroom teacher sends a student who is acting out to the office for accountability, it sends a clear message to the remaining class members that their teacher is unable to manage the room's security, and their anxiety level escalates. The educational leaders of every school are essential in empowering and supporting classroom teachers in developing and trusting their personal skills for sustaining emotional security in learning environments.

Successful leadership today requires school systems to reach beyond their physical plants and playgrounds to the community. Schools alone cannot resolve the issues of troubling behavior, unacceptable achievement, and high dropout rates. Collaboration with community medical and mental health agencies and organizations will help generate a supportive base for the educational changes that will have to be initiated in order for stressed and anxious learners to meet academic and citizenship standards.

Area universities and colleges can explain the neurological basis for education reform to the local media and community organizations so vital to maintaining district voter support. Education leaders who initiate cross-disciplinary collaborations will increase the chances that staff and the parents will implement and reinforce their district's policy changes. Informational outreach between school personnel, parent-teacher organizations, and the area faith community will help generate community support.

Parents, especially the parents of stressed and anxious students, will present the greatest challenge to any changes in school policy or protocols. For some of these parents, the topic of school does not evoke pleasant or satisfying childhood memories. Some of them have never been afforded the opportunity to transform their own shame and sense of helplessness from childhood experiences.

The decision to place visibly armed police officers within a school building needs to be evaluated within this context. This is especially important in neighborhoods where abiding attitudes of trust do not exist between police and youth. The presence of armed, uniformed police within learning environments has as much potential to alarm distressed, anxious students as it has to calm youth fortunate enough never to have been traumatized in their lifetime. Balancing the strategies selected with the full range of needs of the total student body is essential for providing sustained safe learning environments for everyone within a school building, children and staff.

Empowering students to participate in a purposeful way in formulating school safety plans is productive from several perspectives. First, it affords students an opportunity to generate a broader sense of ownership of both the issue and the facility. Implementation will be greatly eased and respected.

Second, students know what is going on with fellow students. By incorporating students in the safety planning, student reporting of critical observations and information about a classmate's plans or activities can be framed as a responsible safety gesture, not as ratting. Promoting anonymous reporting of activities by, or rumors about, the behaviors of fellow students has the potential to generate student body suspicions and mistrust which will be perceived as threats by already anxious youth. It may do the opposite of building unity and a sense of community. Therefore, resolutions that respect the integrity of the bonds of community will ultimately reinforce the common goals of achievement and self-direction.

The previous chapter focused on stress reduction within the classroom. Student experiences in other areas of the school greatly affect their stress level within the classroom as well.

An understanding of the fight-or-flight motivation behind impulsive aggressiveness provides educators with an opportunity to promote school safety without sacrificing student achievement. Implementing a policy that responds to the students' need for a sense of emotional security in the early grades, and continuing the policy as they progress through middle school, will enhance the educational experiences of all students and staff.

The need to remove threats from school discipline has implications beyond the acutely anxious students it addresses most directly. As schools across America discovered to their horror in the 1990s, no student or staff member is any safer than the perceived sense of security and inclusion of the most anxious person within the school. Unless everyone feels secure and valued, no one is safe. The term "Safe Schools" will never offer the security parents and the community expect and deserve unless the safety needs of *every* child are honored and taken into consideration (Garbarino & deLara, 2002).

Not even metal detectors will guarantee school safety because guns and knives do not present the crucial danger; futurelessness does. The sense of a foreshortened future is the cause; gun use is the symptom. True safety comes from addressing causes, and futurelessness enters the building undetected within the soul of the student. Focusing on holistic security rather than the imposition of structural security will create safe school communities in which learning and hope thrive.

The crushing effect of losses and trauma becomes intergenerational and compounded for many students, a reality that only enlarges the need for seamless, integrated community awareness and support.

With the current pressure on local schools to raise their achievement test scores comes a need and an opportunity for all the resilient adults in the community to reach out to the parents of the students who are not achieving. Any action that promotes overall school achievement ultimately brings security and stability for every student in the building. Empowering parents to actively participate in generating school climates that reduce the stress and insecurity of all students actually promotes the achievement of their very own children.

Does demanding higher academic achievement mean we are facilitating increased learning for all students, or are we only increasing the drop-out rate as a way of raising the overall achievement scores of school buildings or systems? The question for the field of education to address is whether we are committed to academic achievement for all students or only for those who can benefit from established policies and strategies.

SPECIFIC STRATEGIES FOR OVERALL SECURITY AND A SENSE OF SAFETY THROUGHOUT THE SCHOOL BUILDING

All students have a right to feel safe and be safe throughout the building and on school grounds. What happens in the halls, cafeteria, and restrooms affects the learning process in classrooms. Students' experiences in the gym, locker rooms, and athletic or play areas circulate back to the classrooms. Adults responsible for maintaining safe schools can take the following measures:

Confer with student council and parents on safety assurance during bus rides.

Consult with staff to schedule announcements when they will be least intrusive.

Explore alternative ways to deliver announcements to staff (e.g., beepers, cell phones).

Hall monitoring: Have many adults present at class change times. Consider parent volunteers. Place an adult in or near less-used areas, where students can be vulnerable. Conduct surveys on where students are secure and insecure throughout the building (Bean, 1999).

Strategize with staff on ways to reduce noise in the cafeteria. Rule out whistles, megaphones, and adult yelling. Consider adding sound-absorbent materials. Confer with student councils.

Quiet room: Designate a small room or area near the school nurse's office where a student can come to regain self-control and composure in privacy for a designated amount of time (20 to 30 minutes). The room door must remain open.

Provide adult monitoring of gym locker rooms whenever they are in use.

Confer with student council on ways to ensure safety in restrooms at all times.

Provide a locked suggestion box in the cafeteria, gym, or office so that students can offer feedback, make requests, and contribute suggestions.

STRATEGIES SPECIFICALLY FOR MIDDLE SCHOOLS

To reduce transition stress, consider assigning a team of teachers for core curriculum subjects and having the teachers, instead of the students, move from room to room.

Consider establishing a set time of 20 to 30 minutes each day when all students meet with an assigned staff person in groups or clans of five or six. These sessions would ensure an anchoring of every student to an adult for the purpose of formulating deep relationships. The mentoring adult would remain with the group throughout the members' years in that building. This project would require the inclusion of all appropriate adults who are willing: office staff, nurse, counselors, parent-teacher aides, and so on.

To ensure stronger adult-student relationships and a sense of connectedness, consider subdividing large schools into contiguous units for 250 to 300 students maximum. However, be aware that recent research indicates merely reducing school size cannot guarantee academic and behavioral improvements. Structural alterations must be combined with the transformation activities for recovery offered in this book to increase the possibilities of better learning and better behavior.

Implementing a buddy program for all students in the incoming grade could have a stabilizing impact on school climate and achievement. All students for whom an individual educational plan has been created would benefit from a buddy program in addition to activities that reduce stress and helplessness. The many medical treatments some students with individual educational plans have experienced can be traumatizing.

SUPPORTS FOR REENTERING STUDENTS

Schools have authentic opportunities to reduce stress and address student vulnerabilities and security needs at times of change or transition. Through collaborations with social service agencies and the school's own student services, provide debriefings and support services for students returning to school after the following events:

Fires at their dwelling or home

Natural disasters

Hospitalization of student or a close family member

Homicide of a family member or friend

Traumatic death and funeral of a family member or friend

Sentencing of a student in a detention center

Arrest or incarceration of a close family member

Foster care placement of student

A stay in a homeless shelter

A stay in a domestic violence center

A drug raid at the student's dwelling

Reentering often results in further marginalization or rejection for vulnerable students. Rejection can easily become psychological cancer, according to William Pollack (1998).

Some of the situations listed above would require collaboration and communication between schools, police, courts, and child protective services.

Teachers can also advocate for a buddy program for all new students or those reentering after lengthy absences or reassignments for health or remedial reasons.

SUPPORTS FOR NEW OR TRANSFERRING STUDENTS

Nearly two thirds of students in the United States transfer at least once during their schooling. Family mobility is part of the changed childhood experienced by many youngsters. However, not all transfers are because of change of residence, a particularly perplexing issue for urban districts.

A single change of residence during Grades 8–12 increases the chances a child will not graduate. Whether the transfer was initiated by the student or the school administration, the impact is counterproductive.

Relocations are common and frequent for children in urban schools. Often these are children who have already experienced repeated losses and separations. Constructing class photo albums early in the year helps students gain a sense of belonging and helps greatly, as does making good-bye cards when someone moves.

Immigrant students most definitely would benefit from personal support. Schools could provide such linkage and support through a buddy system with a student in an upper grade. The advantages of a buddy program are doubled for the school because both students experience enhanced self-confidence and empathy.

The current increase in refugees coming to the United States from war-ravaged homelands means some students are bringing to their schools deep and pervasive traumas that extend far beyond the challenges of acculturation. In addition to the poverty issues many of them confront, these immigrant youngsters are straddling conflicting cultures: the culture of their very stressed parents and the culture of their new school. This conflict adds stress on top of stress.

The mental health issues presented by these students may be intense and may require bilingual counseling services. Although they probably will require professional counseling services, these students can nevertheless benefit from the trauma transformation activities offered in this book, which will support and reinforce their ongoing recovery process and enhance their adjustments to their new school culture.

SUSPENSION AND EXPULSION POLICIES

Our nation's historical focus on public schools as a means of providing an education for all remains the soul of our democracy. How can we achieve that exemplary goal when large numbers of already alienated students are denied participation as the result of being suspended or expelled? School threats, rejections, and vulnerabilities, whether real or perceived, are compounded for these students by the very real dangers of street violence. Suspended youth rarely spend their days in safe isolation within their dwellings.

Threats, including the threat of suspension, may have been an effective disciplinary tool with well-nurtured, unstressed students. The world children are actually living in has changed although adults' expectations and understanding have altered little, especially regarding behavior. But why should we expect to scare children into appropriate behavior when today's youngsters live with greater real fears than some of us have experienced in a lifetime?

Much of the behavior that culminates in suspensions or expulsions is not singular incidents that take place in a vacuum. More often than not, the troubled and troubling youngster has been sending up repeated red flags or calls for help, but the messages have been misinterpreted or ignored. No school system that is committed to safety can afford to ignore the emotional and social needs of angry and lonely students, especially with the easy availability of guns everywhere in the country!

Attempts to generate shock and fear by using the threat of suspension only exacerbate students' insecurities, rage, and acting-out behavior, creating new, heightened tensions and crises. Schools should provide trauma-specific life interviews for every suspended or expelled student to gain insights into causes, possible resolutions, and beneficial referrals.

Many schools have implemented zero-tolerance policies in recent years. Some of these law enforcement models have contributed to confusing, distrustful learning environments, and some have actually victimized students needlessly. Some may even have contributed to school violence, according to Irwin A. Hyman (Hyman & Snook, 1999). Because of the inherent threats such policies can trigger—anxiety and, ultimately, the survival reaction—in already overstressed youth, these policies can generate a misdirected need for revenge despite the lack of direct relationship between the anxious student and any of the victims. The needs of anxious, stressed students who cannot cope with perceived rejections for inclusion are real. Their actions are not just a means of getting attention.

The tragic and terrorizing attacks of September 11, 2001, have caused students and adults across the nation to struggle with grief, fear, and overwhelming uncertainty. For many of America's youngsters, school became a sanctuary where they could process their feelings because their parents were temporarily emotionally unavailable as they dealt with their own sense of helplessness. Some schools were able to facilitate students in this essential process; others ordered teachers not to bring up the subject. It would be a grievous wrong if educators failed to recognize the significance of that horrendous learning experience and did not vow to acquire the essential debriefing skills.

Meeting the valid need for trauma-specific intervention months, even years, following a tragic event may be a challenge for a school system, philosophically as well as fiscally. The initial community outpouring of assistance and support is essential, but justifying the need for long-term services may require an information campaign before the budgetary request. Such a campaign could be turned into an opportunity to increase community awareness that posttraumatic or unresolved trauma behaviors may lie hidden for a year or more after a terrifying event. Media coverage of tragic events in other schools across the nation will trigger recurrences of such trauma reactions, requiring a repeated round of interventions. The willingness to provide ongoing opportunities for trauma-defusing interventions can avert the acting-out behaviors that are easily misinterpreted as possible acts of aggression by already insecure students reacting to news coverage of tragic events. Unfortunately, such incidents of traumatized students' activated alarm responses, which are a cry for security, have resulted in punitive reactions by school administrations that increase anxiety and violate the individual civil rights of students with emotional security needs. Ultimately, such school climate challenges can inadvertently result in altering the sense of security for all students. Revenge is an unfortunate symptom of the help-lessness of traumatized youngsters that can put every person in the school at risk.

It is critically important for any school system intending to adopt the zero-tolerance model to first establish a clear, unified definition of what does and does not constitute a verbal or physical threat. Precise definitions of teasing, bullying, and harassment are essential to protect the integrity of the school system and individual students.

CRISIS PREPARATION

Anita Walker, crisis intervention coordinator for Oklahoma City Public Schools, can attest from tragic experience that the best time to prepare a crisis plan is *before* the need for one is urgent. In a severe crisis, not only are the students traumatized; so are most of the staff, and the sense of community is tragically ruptured, as it certainly was in Manhattan on September 11, 2001.

In a presentation at the TLC Institute in Grosse Pointe Woods, Michigan, Walker offered the most compelling validation for thorough staff preparation when she related how teachers in Oklahoma now implore their system not to leave them untrained in helping children with grief. In a major crisis, the schools may be the only emotional refuge available to the children. One of the insights gleaned from addressing the needs of students after the tragic Oklahoma City bombing is to focus directly on what children need to have happen so that they can feel safe; in other words, to give their fears a voice.

Walker urged schools to be prepared to deal with the hurts and internal scars of previously wounded children, which reopen when there is a high-profile national or local tragic or scary event. She advocates these emotional needs be addressed, defused, and transformed consistently, thereby reducing the potential that frightening events will trigger survival reactions that prove harmful to the students and others in the school community.

The necessity of being prepared to respond to the grief and fears of the student body within every community in the country has become painfully obvious in recent decades. Staff members, parents, or citizens not directly involved in local schools would be performing a vital service by advocating that a crisis plan be put in place. Crisis plans that address the complete physical safety and possible medical needs of students and staff might be easily agreed upon. Reaching consensus on a plan to meet their trauma needs may require thoughtful dedication, particularly when planning for the children's needs (Steele, 1998).

A complete crisis plan will provide debriefing models and designate trained consultants from collaborating agencies. Recruitment and training for the schools' own crisis teams will need to be provided.

William Steele has suggested the model include an operational plan for the entire staff, to be initiated on the first day of the crisis, with a follow-up in three to five days, assessed depending on the duration of the event. Steele strongly advises this training be conducted by an experienced consultant from outside the school system, someone unknown to all staff members. An operational debriefing may last about an hour and be used to evaluate the current status of staff and students, clarify rumors, and determine the needs for immediate support. Alerting staff to possible evolving situational needs and identifying resources or additional support systems would be productive. The staff should be debriefed during every stage of any investigation in order to determine causes or facts. The primary goal of this training is to stabilize and prepare staff to meet the students' needs the next day.

Classroom debriefings for all grades need to be conducted as soon as possible by the crisis team or a staff team and should be less than an hour in length. The purpose of the debriefings is to serve as a barometer regarding students' reactions, concerns, and needs while also answering their questions and providing factual information. Such debriefings offer opportunities to normalize students' reactions and prepare them for what to expect, along with what they can do for themselves and others. Sources of additional help can be shared, along with upcoming related events or activities such as community support gatherings or memorials.

Students with the most direct traumatic exposure may have more intense needs and require age-specific responses from the school's staff or a crisis team. Upper elementary and middle school students with direct exposure may benefit from small-group debriefings a week or even months later, as needed. The purpose of these sessions is to provide relief and promote healing by reviewing what happened, identifying the most difficult part of the event to remember, and discussing what has been done to help students feel safer. The goal of these debriefings is to normalize students' reactions to an abnormal or unusual event. Clarifications about related issues, what to expect, and the support students require may be needed in the coming weeks and months. Debriefers should address referral issues at these sessions.

Elementary students who were directly exposed need sessions that fulfill the same purposes but are never longer than an hour and include storytelling and opportunities to draw during the session.

Critical situations may require small-group debriefings for the debriefers and crisis teams. These situations need an outside consultant.

Complete guidelines for all these debriefing components are included in *Trauma Debriefing for Schools and Agencies*, by William Steele (1998).

There seems to be no consensus on whether a school should practice a building-wide crisis drill. One proactive alternative that could be instituted is to change the term "Fire Drill" to "Safety Drill."

CONFLICT AND ANGER MANAGEMENT

There has been a tremendous focus since the 1990s on teaching conflict and anger management to prevent altercations and improve school climate or safety. These are valuable skills that can greatly enhance children's well-being in school and throughout life.

The evidence presented in Chapters 1 and 2 about the brain changes resulting from persistent threatening experiences in childhood indicates that violence is not "learned" in the true sense of learning but is a survival maladaptation. It would seem probable that when violent behaviors were not acquired through a learning process, the youngsters cannot be successfully "taught" a more constructive alternative, that is, not before the memories and perceptions of being helpless and powerless have been transformed.

Teaching conflict and anger management skills is purposeful and productive for all students, but stressed, anxious children and youth can apply them only when they feel safe and secure. These successes will enhance the goal of safe schools but may bring a new form of vulnerability to an already troubled youth. When these youngsters sense danger, their neuroprogrammed survival reaction of impulsive aggression will erupt, much to the surprise of the student trained in conflict management. Youth counselors report the dismay and shock their clients express over having lashed out and not understanding why; they feel betrayed by their own bodies and hopeless about their ability to change.

The sincere goal of schools to build the skills of students to resolve personal or social conflicts and improve school climate is valid. Ensuring that students can implement these valued skills, even when they perceive a threat, requires that youngsters must first dissipate and transform any buried memories of helplessness that may exist. The healing activities offered in this book are essential and integral to effective anger and conflict management programs.

A valuable resource for teachers of eighth grade is *Conflict Resolution in American History: Lessons From the Past, Lessons for Today,* available from Peace Education, 1900 Biscayne Blvd., Miami, FL 33132; phone: (800) 749-8838; URL: www.PeaceEducation .com.

VIOLENCE PREVENTION STRATEGIES

Early Prevention

Prevention and intervention cannot really be separated. The reality that young children possess an innate capacity to recover and stabilize is a saving grace that deserves attention but does not eliminate the need for early prevention or intervention. The critical hurdle is interrupting the cycle between the perception of threat and an aggressive response. This interruption should free the brain from the survival mode so students can pause and choose their response (Niehoff, 1999).

Empirical evidence suggests the academic achievement of these children will also be at risk, attesting to the urgency of early interventions. Waiting for children to outgrow these behaviors merely compounds the risks for the youngsters and their future as well as the safety of the students, classmates, and teachers.

School nurses can play an important role in a school's plan to sensitively monitor students reeling from the effects of a tragic, traumatizing experience. Following specialized training in children's trauma, nurses will be able to recognize the physiological effects and valid somatic complaints that accompany trauma. Through records of visits to their office, nurses may be in the best position of all staff for detecting trauma cues and assisting the classroom teachers in selecting supportive responses.

Prevention programs can reduce the need for punishment. A prevention focus requires that all staff, including playground and lunchroom personnel, understand structural changes in brain development, trauma, and the behaviors presented by traumatized children. The impact of the school's discipline policy on anxious children would need to be evaluated in designing any prevention program. Guidelines should allow for flexible responses to students' need to move around, and even leave the classroom, when an intrusive memory overtakes them.

Bullying

Responding to the early presentation of bullying and teasing is a way of preventing violence in the future. Identifying and effectively intervening in bullying and harassing incidents can reduce or eliminate a significant proportion of school violence. Since victimizers almost always have been victimized, interventions will need to address the original hurts or causes, not merely the symptomatic behaviors. The goal of long-term bullying intervention is to transform the fear, shame, or sense of rejection, not drive it deeper into hiding. Bullying prevention must include addressing and resolving the perceptions of helplessness for both the victim and the instigator.

An effort to incorporate bully prevention in education will have to include parents and extend to the community to be effective. Establishing a solid foundation for a school program can begin with an informational evening session that clarifies the definitions of teasing, name-calling, taunting, bullying, race-baiting, and assault. Without parental and community buy-in, implementing a program may become factious. Inviting area clergy and recreation program leaders and coaches will increase community cooperation. Various materials are available in *Sticks and Stones*, by Katherine J. Kocs (see details below).

Bullying not only creates fear and factions within the student body; it can cause some victims to consider violent retribution, especially when they sense the staff is unprepared or unwilling to intervene. Chronic victims can become so desperate that they inflict violence on themselves. Student suicide and persistent bullying are associated (Elias & Zins, 2003).

Many students state that they have spoken to adults in their school about being bullied or harassed but received no response or support (Garbarino & deLara, 2002). If adults fail to respond or to take the psychological impact of bullying seriously, how can students identify bullying behaviors as abusive? Hence, students deduce that nothing will change and that their situation is hopeless. Garbarino and deLara claim only 25 percent of students believe adults are aware of anyone making their school unsafe. Safety emerges out of a sense that caring adults are willing to use their authority to help bring about solutions.

Adults are ultimately responsible for maintaining safe schools. Schools, which operate as a system, tend to work toward maintaining the system. Systems discourage change by rewarding conformity. Unfortunately, this pattern often leads to scapegoating of those who cannot conform. Scapegoats are a clue that the system is not a healthy one. Slogans and programs that do not change the underlying school culture and social environment will not succeed in preventing bullying or harassment.

Many published programs for bullying prevention focus primarily on empowering vulnerable students to be more assertive. Such formats certainly can be helpful, but they address only half of the problem. Until the root causes of bullying have been addressed, no school will have resolved the issue; the bully simply finds new peers to victimize in other locations.

When the responsibility for preventing bullying is thrust onto the vulnerable, the student body recognizes that the adults are not able to maintain safe environments and actually don't know what to do other than punish after the fact. Bullying is a symptom and will not end until the cause is resolved and a more appropriate behavior pattern established.

Bullying behaviors are directly correlated to experiencing family violence (Kagan, 2004). Youngsters who had to learn that aggression is essential for self-preservation recognize that it works in certain situations. When these child-victims later see similar terror and helplessness on the faces of those they have taunted, the aggressors experience some relief from their own memories of fear. The resulting sense of power and mastery can be very satisfying; so much so that it even offsets the rejection and punishments that may follow.

How can schools provide an alternative form of relief to the satisfaction a victim-bully gets from generating fear in a targeted victim? According to Kagan (2004), the relief the bully senses far exceeds the effects of any restrictions or disciplinary actions that may be implemented.

Symbolic opportunities to replace the relief achieved through bullying offer proactive ways to change the unacceptable behavior. The following value-clarification game can serve as such a tool.

For the activity "Why Students Need to Feel Safe in School," photocopy the accompanying game board and the page of cards. Cut apart the cards and ask the victim-bully to prioritize the cards on the game board. The student must indicate what he or she would add to the wild card, that is, what seems to be missing from the choices.

The most productive way to use the game is in one-on-one counseling by the school counselor, social worker, or a trusted teacher. As the student looks down at the game board and nears completion, the adult should gently pose questions related to the cards and their placement and ask what the terms or conditions on the cards mean to the student.

The adult should continue by asking how a student might know that the desired policy or guideline has been put in place. What specifics would tell the student that he or she could trust the guidelines and that the staff was following the principles? What suggestions would the student like to make that would increase his or her sense of safety and security?

In follow-up sessions, the adult can engage the victim-bully student in creating guidelines for assuring safety for *all* students in the halls, restrooms, cafeteria, and playground. The discussion can be expanded to other areas of the school plant and to specifics for younger students. The victim-bully students can be asked where they would like to share these guidelines: the student council, the principal, the gym teacher, and any others. Would they like to be trained in conflict mediation? They can also be engaged in some of the healing activities offered in earlier chapters of this book.

Exclusion is a form of bullying and turns a student into both a victim and a bully. Sanctioned rejection is psychological maltreatment and can trigger the residue of helplessness left over from childhood experiences. Bullies act out of their own sadness and fears with the intent of reclaiming dignity—and getting even. Revenge, however, does not heal their despair. Empowerment is the antidote for helplessness, providing the bully with a way to contribute and feel valued.

The students who look the least helpless may in fact feel the most helpless, according to Garbarino and deLara (2002). Adults must recognize the connection

BECAUSE THEY CAN'T PROTECT THEMSELVES	**IN ORDER TO EXPERIENCE RESPECT FROM OTHERS**
IN ORDER TO UNDERSTAND AND EXPERIENCE WHAT TRUST IS	**TO UNDERSTAND DEMOCRACY**
SO THEY CAN CONCENTRATE ON LEARNING	**TO UNDERSTAND THE IMPORTANCE OF RULES**
TO FEEL VALUED	**TO APPRECIATE SECURITY**
BECAUSE EVERY STUDENT DESERVES TO FEEL SAFE	**TO GAIN CONFIDENCE IN THEMSELVES**
WILD CARD	**BECAUSE IT MAY BE THE ONLY PLACE WHERE THEY CAN FEEL SAFE**

Why Students Need to Feel Safe in School

1	7
2	8
3	9
4	10
5	11
6	12

between students who feel helpless and unsafe at school and those who fail, become troublemakers, and drop out.

A number of good resources on bullying are available. Books include the following:

Stein, N., Sjostrom, L., & Mullin-Rindler, N. (1996). *Bullyproofing Your School: A Teacher's Guide on Teasing and Bullying for Use With 4th and 5th Grade Students.* Wellesley, MA: Wellesley College Center for Research on Women.

Beane, A. (1999). *Bully Free Classroom.* Minneapolis, MN: Free Spirit Publishing.

Videos include the following:

Broken Toy
c/o Thomas Brown
P.O. Box 2219
Zanesville, OH 43702-2219

Let's Get Real
c/o Women's Educational Media
2180 Bryant Street
San Francisco, CA 44110
www.womedia.org

Second Step
Committee for Children
Phone: (800) 634-4449

Kocs, K. J. (1999). *Sticks and Stones: Changing the Dynamics of Bullying and Youth Violence.* Madison, WI: University of Wisconsin Health Services.

The following teaching guides are published by Wellesley College Center for Research on Women, Education Equity Concepts, and NEA Professional Library:

Flirting or Hurting? A Teacher's Guide on Student-to-Student Sexual Harassment in Schools. (1994). For Grades 6 and up.

Gender Violence/Gender Justice: An Interdisciplinary Teaching Guide for Teachers of English, Literature, Social Studies, Health, Family and Consumer Sciences. (1999). For Grades 7 and up.

Student books:

Ludwig, T. (2003). *My Secret Bully.* Ashland, OR: RiverWood Books.

Moss, P. (2004). *Say Something.* Gardiner, MA: Tilbury House.

Inclusion

All students need to feel recognized and included; the hicks, Goths, preppies, and athletes all have to have a voice.

To be socially ostracized by classmates is interpreted by traumatized children as rejection (Garbarino & deLara, 2002; Karr-Morse & Wiley, 1997). Although that pattern often has its beginnings during the early elementary grades, the effects on personal identity take on deeper, more critical meaning during puberty and adolescence. Schools do not and should not determine the social groupings of students. But schools do have a unique opportunity, through school clubs and extracurricular activities, to avert the marginalization and social ostracism of students who may not fit the prevailing definition of mainstream.

School clubs that combine or overlap interests and hobbies in a new or alternative configuration could provide a way to reach marginalized students before they become alienated. Hopefully such clubs could offer a means for vulnerable students to connect before they drop out or join a gang for acceptance and social identity. Here are several suggestions:

Exploring music styles and their effects on history and culture

Exploring movies and movie production and their effects on history and culture

The Detroit Club, for examining car design and its effects on history, economics, and ecology

The Comic Book Club, for examining the history and styles of comics and their creation

The Art of Tattoos, for exploring the history, cultural meanings, and creation of tattooing

Gangs and gang participation are not a direct responsibility of school systems; maintaining safe learning environments for *all* students is. Schools are parts of communities, and youth who join gangs represent opportunities lost to the entire community. Gang participation is a symptom, not a cause, of alienated and terrified youth who feel no hope.

Gang participation is symptomatic of the maladaptations children and youth make to find some sense of identity, connectedness, and security. To proactively prevent young people from joining gangs and dropping out of school, schools must create early academic success through reducing students' stress, which in turn promotes inclusion and generates hope.

Similarly, drug use, guns, and gun ownership are community issues. Again, schools are an integral part of the community and have the opportunity to address the causes through the proactive, preventative alternatives and strategies outlined in this chapter. Programs like DARE and Eddie Eagle do not proactively address causes; they primarily address symptoms.

Restorative Justice

The primary reaction of American schools to school violence and disruptive behavior is punishment. However, many state constitutions mandate that their schools provide an education to all the state's children. It is regrettable that many of the nation's schools fail to take advantage of those teachable moments prompted by an unacceptable incident to build solutions that constructively serve everyone involved.

Punishment does not "teach" solutions; it does not hold offenders accountable for the disruption and harm they have caused, and it does not afford victims an opportunity to have their needs responded to. The intent of restorative justice, on the other hand, is to repair the harm done and restore a sense of safe community; it reintegrates the offender into the school community and the educational program.

Restorative justice offers offenders a way to make things right, and it gives victims a voice in what needs to happen so safety can be restored. The process leads perpetrators to address root causes and internalize alternative, productive ways to resolve them, and it leads to lower recidivism.

Education in restorative justice involves the entire school community, including parents. The process, implemented by a trained team of facilitators, becomes an additional tool in a school's traditional disciplinary system.

Conferences are similar to mediations but include everyone affected by the action or event, including the parents of both the victim and the offender. Perpetrators hear exactly how their offense has affected everyone and what they need to do to rebuild a sense of community within the school. The process builds lasting solutions.

Types of cases appropriate for restorative justice include the following:

Theft

Graffiti and other vandalism

Bullying and harassment

Minor physical assault

Verbal assault

Truancy

Unintentional injury

Disruptive behaviors

Defiance of authority

Resource for restorative justice:

Colorado School Mediation Project
2885 Aurora Avenue, Suite 13
Boulder, CO 80303
Phone: (303) 444-7671; Fax: (303) 444-7247
URL: www.csmp.org
A video is available for $40.00 plus postage.

General resources and Web sites:

Students Against Violence Everywhere (SAVE)
Phone: (866) 343-SAVE
URLs: www.nationalsave.org, www.cde.ca.gov/spbranch/safetylinks.asp

Institute for the Study and Prevention of Violence, Kent State University
Phone: (330) 672-7917
URL: http://dept.kent.edu/violence

Ebased Prevention
URL: www.ebasedprevention.org

Ohio Resource Network
Phone: (800) 788-7254
URL: dept.kent.edu/violence

The Ohio Commission on Dispute Resolution and Conflict Management
Phone: (614) 752-9595
URL: www.state.oh.us/cdr/

Committee for Children
Phone: (800) 634-4449
URL: www.cfchildren.org
This group offers a free CD explaining its program "Steps to Respect."

9

Meaningful Change in the U.S. Education System

The topic of educational reform has surfaced frequently throughout the nation during the past decade. While there has been tremendous legislative focus on educational policy and standards, there has not been a corresponding emphasis on the most significant component of America's schools: the students and their needs.

Seasoned educators have observed a continuous ebb and flow of catchwords and trends. The promise of cooperative education a generation ago has all but vanished as more and more emphasis is placed on test scores and school ratings, along with consequences for failing to meet established standards. A climate of competition and stress permeates nearly all schools, making the laudable goals even more unattainable.

The question of how to reach and teach today's students continues to be absent from the elevated focus on curriculum and academics. The big goal of improving the staggeringly disappointing test scores in so many schools remains elusive despite the best intentions. Education policymakers have tweaked just about everything there is to tweak, with one glaring exception: matching the academic delivery system to the actual learning needs of today's students—youngsters who are living in a world very different from the one their dedicated teachers and principals grew up in.

The information from neurobiological research presented in this volume dramatically challenges the assumptions and standard practices that have been the basis of the teaching practices and school policy that have been accepted for decades. The changes needed in best practices are drastic, and they come at a time when every educator in America is feeling relentless pressure to produce elevated test scores.

INITIATING CHANGE FROM THE GROUND UP

Change is never comfortable, and when one's very own employment contract is caught in the balance, change is arduous. Unless there is consensus in an entire district to consider major changes, it is unlikely individual teachers will be able to initiate unified reform of any significance.

Where and how, then, might change begin? Many professionals in a wide range of fields have observed that lasting, meaningful change tends to grow from the bottom up rather than descend from the top. It takes longer, but such a thrust will have the advantage of the dedication and strength of committed practitioners to sustain actual implementation. Individual teachers can find this process both empowering and energizing.

One teacher's initiating the communication and classroom strategies suggested throughout this book can generate academic advances in one classroom regardless of student experiences in other settings within a school. Naturally, student advances would climb if similar strategies were implemented throughout the school by all staff, but they can start in one class.

Word of mouth can be very powerful, and eventually fellow staff will take note of accelerated achievements and reduced misbehavior in classrooms where emotional security has been generated. Colleagues take note of teachers who appear to have sustained motivation and that wondrous sense of professional fulfillment. After all, didn't we become educators because we believed we could make a difference in the lives of students? Opportunities to comment and share strategies happen regularly in the teachers' lounge. Teacher-to-teacher mentoring is powerful.

GENERATING SUPPORT

All teachers and educators need deep and sustained support; emotional and psychological support from parents and voters is essential, but support from the local medical, mental health, juvenile justice, and commercial communities is also vital. Schools do not operate in a vacuum. However, these entities cannot know what they don't know about children's capacity to learn unless educators inform the public discourse on this issue. Educators are the ones best qualified to determine the future of public education.

Maintaining personal awareness of the emerging neurobiological research that reveals how students learn and manage their behavior can reinforce educators' opportunities to enlist community support for change. As complicated as this research may seem to be, it holds the key to future change and success. Several Web sites mentioned in previous chapters offer updated information that will support educators in generating grassroots advocacy.

Enlisting local print and electronic media to support the changes necessary to reach and teach today's students can be very challenging but also very productive. Local news and editorials will reflect the information journalists are aware of. Herein lies an opportunity for administrators and teachers to give reporters the information essential for generating community support for educational change.

Community leaders are very aware of the challenges facing education systems locally and nationally. These entities are also aware that changes have to evolve for the sustained viability of their community's stability and economic growth, and they are seeking constructive options. This search for options offers educators a true opportunity. As professionals, educators not only can offer these options; we have a responsibility to offer them despite the burdens of stress inherent in doing so.

Reaching out to local and state college and university researchers in behavioral pediatrics and neurobiology for their persuasive support can be very effective. Cross-disciplinary influence for crucial educational reform can build community consensus and commitment.

Educators at all levels, kindergarten through postgraduate, have to take back the crucial responsibility of setting the direction of public education; we must make our voices heard.

Resource A:
Crossword Puzzles

These crossword puzzles may be photocopied for student use.

Note: These puzzles were created with software available online. For a fee, you can easily create additional crossword puzzles for your students by going to www.CrosswordWeaver.com. A free demo is available on this Web site.

PUZZLE 1

Across

3 To recover from a shocking loss, in part

8 What all youngsters need from someone they can trust

9 What someone whose safety is in peril may need to do

10 To be able to come to; to open and receive

12 Vocal sounds that can trigger memories

14 What one can do to reduce anxiety and stress

15 The primary urge for all people

20 Extends loving help and support

21 What youngsters often claim while it was an adult who was responsible

22 The perceived feeling or sense that follows a shocking loss or terror

23 To behave suddenly out of fear, not as the result of choice

26 What someone who has been mistreated finds hard to do

27 What every child or person has a right to experience after an injustice

28 What needs to happen to memories of loss

Down

1 What children who have healed their feelings after mistreatment can do once again

2 To take in air freely; hard to do when anxious but a way to relax

4 What we often want to do with troubling feelings or memories

5 Experience being denied when separated from someone or something important

6 What youngsters who have recovered from loss or mistreatment can once again believe in

7 What people do if they don't want to be found and want to stay safe

11 A condition caused by extreme pressure

13 How one can feel when surprised or shocked by a loss

16 The ability to see into issues or problems and understand

17 A person who has been mistreated

18 The base cause of most aggressive behaviors

19 Acts of aggression that can cause harm to others or self

24 What frightened youngsters have a hard time finding

25 How many young people remain after experiencing or witnessing injustice

PUZZLE 1

PUZZLE 2

Across

2 A budding, new thought
3 Abbreviation for socially exciting
5 A physical action that is sometimes necessary for safety
6 Super, elevated actions, sometimes for purposes of survival
8 Being true and faithful by choice
9 A form of activity that can bring renewal and satisfaction
10 What lots of people wish could happen to personal hurts
11 The ability to be very good at doing something
14 The center of a storm
18 Having been treated aggressively, resulting in a sense of helplessness and fear
19 The kind of thoughts or memories that keep coming back
21 The ability to sense what another is feeling
24 Constant laboring or working
26 Extremely angry or engraged
28 The need to _____ can cause feelings of pressure
30 The internal sense of embarrassment imposed by someone more powerful
33 To experience a stinging sensation
34 To be in control of one's emotions
35 The essential capacity to create visions of one's future

Down

1 A female student
2 Extreme anger
3 The desired state of optimism, essential for working toward the future
4 The process of absorbing: we take _____
5 To breathe deeply and reduce stress
6 To pay attention, be alert
7 Guaranteed, given standards of treatment available to all human beings regardless of age, gender, race, or class
8 Experiences of deprivation, separation, and disconnection
12 A skill or capacity to succeed
13 An agreeable response a youngster can make when feeling safe
15 To reclaim one's integrity and honor
16 What we sometimes do with our memories
17 The feeling caused by frustration or shock
20 An instrument that can be used to accomplish a task
22 The verbal or physical actions by another that can be perceived to be intended to harm
23 Light, absorbent paper
25 Internal strength that can inspire others
27 Delicate, soft, and satisfying
29 Having personal energy in great amounts
31 Past tense of "eat"
32 Process of taking in food

PUZZLE 2

PUZZLE 3

Across

6 Extreme anger combined with a loss
8 Reference to information that may be overvalued, even contrived
11 Opportunities to meet with relatives; can cause excitement or anxiety
13 Pictures of bloody actions
14 Abbreviation for an information storage disk
15 Feeling mixed up and uncertain
17 The capacity to know internally, intuitively
19 To carry on verbally, loudly, and consistently
23 The number of years that make a decade
26 To perform a physical action automatically, not because of rational thought
28 Different; does not fit into the whole
29 To struggle with a problem or issue
30 A statement that can require courage to say
31 A harsh, strong taste, aroma, or memory
33 A female deer
34 The statement or question said over and over by friends and relatives of someone victimized or hurt accidentally
36 An experience that can teach
39 The process of communicating verbally but not always with ease
40 The process that allows one not to remember
41 The complete internal awareness of self, thoughts, and emotions
42 A mental vision that takes place when sleeping
44 A personality trait that can bring a sense of distance from one's pain
45 Physical contact that can be pleasant or unwanted

Down

1 An untruth
2 Drawing or painting; often used to provide inner empowerment
3 Disarray; a confusing mess
4 Escaped quickly; a survival action
5 Extreme fright and fear of being harmed
7 Extreme sadness caused by a major loss
9 To escape in haste
10 What every child absolutely needs in order to grow and develop
12 The exertion of power over another; declaring exactly what can and cannot be done
14 An independent feline
16 What we feel when joy causes us to soar
17 Feelings of grief, unhappiness
18 To take legal action
20 Feeling left out, abandoned
21 The ability to achieve academically with ease
22 Temporary fashion
24 Exceptionally harsh, troublesome, uncomfortable
25 The capacity of childhood experiences to shape a person's understanding of self and trust
27 A quality of voice that generates emotional meanings
32 The process that brings internal release of stress and discomfort
35 An instrument on police, fire, and emergency vehicles that can trigger memories of scary events
37 To look for, explore, and desperately want to find
38 To turn away; ward off
40 Unclear, in a daze; often follows a shocking loss
43 An affectionate name for one's mother

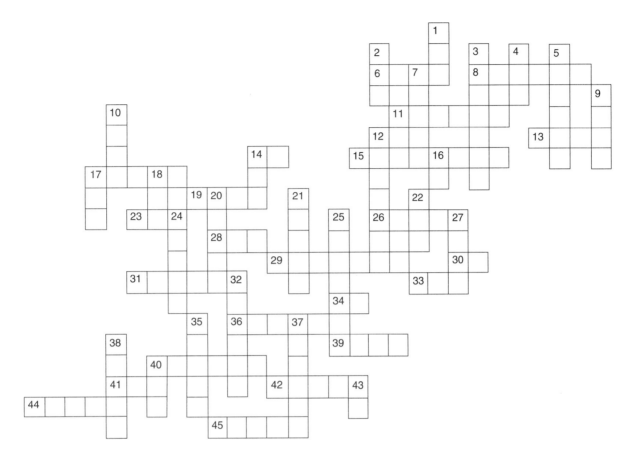

PUZZLE 3

PUZZLE 4

Across

4 A mistake, often accompanied by regrets
5 To gain understanding and skills
8 The state of being in full harmony with oneself and others; living in trust and justice
9 A form of competition
12 To cause to feel reborn; invigorate
13 The capacity to allow oneself to remember
15 A desired state of mind and feeling of hope
16 The essential development task of all youngsters, which requires emotional security
17 What we hope the good and gentle will do
18 To see, track; go after help
20 Deliberate attempts to avert, not encounter
24 The distinctive personality of a person
26 A kind of literature that can provide deep emotional connections
27 A grouping built on trust and togetherness
28 The ability to rely on the fairness and caring of another; essential for security
29 The act of placing
30 An affectionate term for a youngster
31 The ability to be aware of emotional states or sensations
33 To roam aimlessly, without focus
36 The creative process that can turn something truly ugly into something beautiful
38 The process of recovery; to regain hope and emotional freedom

Down

1 A design for action
2 An essential gas for the breath of life
3 To change direction away from, to avoid
4 Looking forward with assurance
6 The goal of students and athletes
7 A drop of liquid that may express sadness, pain, or joy and can offer relief
9 The way recent new fears may feel
10 Recalling an experience or event with all the emotions that encase it
11 To move with speed, to help or escape
14 The hoped-for relationship between friends
17 A process of externalizing issues that may be difficult to say
18 The internal strength within each and every person
19 A quality that makes each youngster a valued and special person
21 The age-group of young adults
22 Feeling of joyous expectations
23 Doing something new, scary, and possibly confusing
25 How every youngster hopes to be accepted by peers
26 The process of putting away; stuffing
28 What youngsters should do if they have a problem
32 Half of the essential ingredient for new life
34 A poem with elaborate style and feelings
35 The perception of equality and justice
37 A group working together in trust and harmony toward a goal

PUZZLE 4

PUZZLE 5

Across

3 Group of trusted peers
5 When everyone is treated equally, fairly
8 To be secure, free from emotional and physical harm
10 A standard of caring; being responsible and appropriate
12 The process of being moved to achieve or change by a caring person
14 Straying, wandering in search of adventure
15 An enjoyable activity
16 Opposite of past; essential for hope
18 A parent
19 Requirements; what children must experience or receive in order to complete development
22 Being in danger, at risk
25 Feeling safe, emotionally and physically
27 At ease, relaxed, able to take deep breaths and think
29 A great distance
31 To boost; make someone feel stronger
32 Clue to sadness
33 A task that is simple, uncomplicated
35 To feel helpless, lonely, and hopeless
36 Something that keeps growing if not treated, like a bad memory

Down

1 Worn on head
2 The way ideas, perceptions, dreams can seem to be
4 Having capability
6 A positive answer
7 Can bring relief from stress when taken deeply, fully
9 Being physically required by someone with greater power
11 What someone in danger needs
13 A writing tool
15 To be relieved of a burden and able to make choices
16 A body type that can bring negative attention
17 Accessed or opened something buried
20 To send away, get rid of
21 Predetermined events, but which youngsters need to sense they choose or shape in order to have hope
23 One begins a new way of life by turning it over
24 A blockage to overcome in order to complete a task or make progress
26 _____ actions are required when environments are not safe
28 Place of safety and security
30 What adults call the back talk of children who may be feeling powerless
31 A type of memory one wants to forget
34 What can be difficult to do when stressed or anxious

PUZZLE 5

PUZZLE 6

Across

3 A trusted friend

4 Behavior that becomes a repeated pattern

6 The way another or a person with authority can make it possible for a youngster to believe in his or her future

8 An action that requires courage and self-trust

9 An order from another or a person with authority

11 To confuse and divert attention

14 To provide a sense of support and empowerment

15 The efforts needed to accomplish something of importance

16 Friends and others in your age-group

17 To perform a natural action necessary for self-protection

20 What youngsters sometimes need to do when in unsafe situations

21 The body part that directs a person's behavior

23 An action that one person does for another and that brings satisfaction

24 A taxi

25 A statement that youngsters sometimes need to say in new situations

27 An emotion that can grow out of a sense of fear and helplessness

29 A time factor that can hold many memories

30 One's destiny; what every person has a right and responsibility to shape

31 A reaction or sense caused by something unexpected and shocking

32 A kind of memory that can be upsetting

Down

1 The source of one's instinct or internal drive to survive

2 One of the senses that can trigger memories with intensity

3 The effect of stress and high expectations on a person

4 Unpleasant treatment or reactions

5 To perform an action

6 The desired or hoped-for stop or closure

7 A biological description of a person's character or personality

10 A decision that one is free to make

12 Feeling that causes stress

13 An internal sense of personal honor

18 One's ability to pay full attention and not be distracted

19 What a person does to lose weight

20 What someone might say to another to avoid a crisis or consequence

22 The perfect expectation and value

26 The process that allows one to examine something hidden or unknown

27 To pay attention, notice, especially to one's intuition

28 How one can portray being someone different from oneself

PUZZLE 6

PUZZLE 7

Across

2 Hoped-for possibility, something referred to in the future
4 People looked up to, ones who inspire
6 A small circle
8 What is required by strong people when overpowered
9 Vocal speech that is a right and is essential for creating a fair and just world
10 Feelings generated by shame or being treated wrongly
14 What a person with strengths is reported to have
15 Soft as, comforting as
17 The characteristics, needs, and nature of _____ beings
21 Where a person's scariest memories are embedded or locked
22 Be aware, take notice
23 An emotionally powerful need and drive
24 To feel anger because of being wronged
27 To form friendships and relationships
28 To move into, to explore
29 To reduce hazards and avert negative experiences
30 What people willing to empower youth can do
32 Action taken that was necessary to stay safe

Down

1 What every student hopes will be excellent
3 What is needed to work through troubles and memories
5 Not any
7 Physically powerful, challenging, a potential threat
8 A powerful, negative emotion generated by fears and lack of understanding
11 An achievement
12 A standard of caring legality; concern for appropriate treatment
13 To come to someone's aid
14 An essential right that all people need to have respected
16 A healthy, natural feeling that a person can make choices about how to handle
18 To use, employ, or implement
19 The result of listening intently; what youngsters need adults to do more of
20 To take part in a contest
21 Distasteful, harsh, painful; sometimes even between friends
25 What is needed by a person or people in danger
26 To an excessive degree
31 The most important person in your life

PUZZLE 7

PUZZLE 8

Across

1 A cherished goal
6 The way one gets relief in order to let go of hurts
7 What happens to feelings of fear and loneliness
9 The way some hurting youngsters try to feel better
10 How a new student feels on the first day
11 What can help a person deal with anger
14 How one feels when excluded
16 A way of looking at the world that may limit hope because of past experiences
18 The feeling youngsters who care may get when they could not stop an accident
19 A look that can cause discomfort
23 What youngsters need from adults and themselves
24 A strong connection with one we trust
26 How some youngsters feel when they perceive their environment as unsafe
27 How a heart feels when lonely or broken

Down

2 The way every person needs to feel to be whole
3 The work or process needed to feel hopeful again
4 What we do with feelings we do not want to remember
5 The way one feels when understood and respected
8 What every young person needs from others, especially adults
9 The state resulting from mixed feelings
12 What hurting people do with their feelings
13 The way we come to protect our feelings when rejected
15 The feelings that can come when lonely
17 What sometimes happens to opportunities
20 What frightening sounds and sights can bring one who feels powerless
21 To not think about a memory or feeling
22 The feelings caused by a sudden and shocking loss
25 A kind of promise

PUZZLE 8

PUZZLE 9

Across

1 Abbreviation for a beloved extraterrestrial from a movie
3 To keep, store items of special meaning
5 An artistic activity that can help relieve stress and hopelessness
6 To drive, incite, or push
7 Personal inner drive, the power of one's conscience
9 To evade, wish wouldn't happen
11 What is said to be in the veins of someone with no compassion
15 A short illness that one seems to get more often when stressed or anxious
16 Matters of importance to be resolved
18 A strong dislike often based on lack of understanding or unrecognized fears
20 A coating used to preserve
22 Found relief, t support, or comfort
24 What some people want to inflict on another, or groups of others, to even the score, only to find it does not bring relief or recovery
25 To get over, regain normalcy, and let go
26 Make advances, make progress
27 A short word some use that means yes
28 A picture story in one's head while one is asleep; they happen more frequently after one has been shocked
30 The legal process of taking someone to court for wrongdoing
34 What we say to ourselves when we are certain of our capability
35 A ritual that can be dangerous, belittling, distressing
37 Sometimes fictional, sometimes true
39 Part of our system that certain persons can irritate
40 Unseen

Down

2 To link together
3 The act of putting into words; sometimes difficult when feelings are the topic
4 Fashion, trend, or fad
5 Past tense for see, witness
8 A mistruth that can cause hurt, especially when spoken by a trusted person
10 The act of having been saved when in danger
12 To become different, to grow and make different choices
13 An art form that can assist a person coping with stress and distress
14 A legal regulation or decree that can be different for youth compared with adults
17 What it seems persons who are hyper have in excess
19 To have caught sight of
21 People who are easily upset or frightened because of experiences they've had
23 Important tests that can generate stress
25 The act of helping others can be _____
29 Abbreviation for telecommunications with picture and sound, the content of which can be educational or detrimental
31 The collective internal sense of self-worth which no person can take from another
32 A short statement of emotional expression, surprise, triumph, contempt, or satisfaction
33 To eliminate, forget
34 A form of bullying using the Internet and which needs to be reported to stop
36 To move forward by choice
38 Abbreviation for tuberculosis

PUZZLE 9

PUZZLE 10

Across

1 What some put on to hide their hurt or scared feelings
5 What one can do for oneself by helping others
6 A message or memory that can burn inside
8 How one can feel when flooded with hurtful memories
9 What can happen to memories of fear and helplessness when one feels threatened
11 What true and trusted friends need to be
14 What can happen to hurt feelings when one journals or draws them
18 How one can feel after a shocking experience
20 How friends can sometimes be
25 An action that is hard for an insecure person to admit
26 Something one can do for oneself when lonely or hurt
27 A natural drive to be safe, to _____
28 How one can feel for oneself that can be unhelpful unless resolved
29 What can become of one's ability to trust after being rejected and hurt

Down

2 Emotional ones hurt the longest
3 What every youngster has a right to have to the fullest
4 A way to hold others responsible when one feels powerless
6 The process of discovering new meanings or understandings for ourselves
7 The question we ask ourselves over and over after being hurt by another
10 What happens to the talents and potential of youngsters who give up
12 The result of being rejected
13 What every person and his or her future has to offer
15 Being able to stay on track and concentrate, even while hurting
16 Childhood memories of fear keep coming back because they are _____
17 What one can feel after one's anger is resolved
19 What one can choose to do about or in oneself
21 What one feels when accepted and respected
22 One is _____ of one's sense of hope when one feels helpless and alone
23 What can be very hard to when angry or hurt
24 A natural way to release hurting feelings

PUZZLE 10

PUZZLE 11

Across

5 What one does for oneself, not for the one who caused a hurt
7 A trick or deception
8 What every youngster needs others to do
10 The kind of pain caused by rejection
11 The physical expectation socially imposed on girls
12 The way one feels when excluded or rejected
14 An unwritten requirement of behavior from some friends
15 Letting someone else define who we are for better or worse
17 A friend acting arrogant
18 What one who feels all alone may want to do
19 Something all youngsters have a right to shape and decide
21 The inner quality that allows one to think for oneself
22 Why some place blame on others
25 What every person needs to feel about who he or she is
26 Where hurt youngsters need healing
27 The only person who I can honestly be

Down

1 What one does with the hurtful comments of others when one believes them
2 What some do to ensure they are never left out
3 What a group of friends can become
4 What lonely youngsters do with feelings of loneliness
6 When everyone works for the good of the whole, they are _____
9 What one can do with a friend who can't be trusted
13 A safe place where one can feel valued and connected
14 What one can do in private that helps healing
16 What may be socially risky for girls because of other girls
18 What we can do with someone we trust
20 What a youngster's deepest needs and longings may remain
21 What some hurting youngsters try to do for their parents
23 What every youngster has a right to do for himself or herself
24 What hurt youngsters need to do with new dreams

PUZZLE 11

PUZZLE 12

Across

2 A title people who have more power can impose on others
5 A kind of friend
6 The type of friend one needs when being manipulated
8 To develop skills for dealing with stress and anxieties
10 What one feels like when ridiculed
13 How false friends define their mean words
14 A constant concern over not being liked and accepted
16 The actions of a self-centered person
18 An action others may take to embarrass someone
21 The action or style of someone who feels hopeless and helpless
23 A reputation many want and some manipulate for
24 How one feels when one sees no alternatives or choices
25 How we feel when another makes fun of us
26 A school culture issue that tends to generate bullying behaviors
27 Hurtful actions taken by someone who feels he or she has been mistreated
28 What one does when one has a false sense of one's own importance
29 The position taken by one who cannot admit committing a wrong

Down

1 The word adults use to try to excuse unfair actions by a classmate
3 A painful feeling caused or brought on by being called names
4 To allow oneself to tell a trusted person about one's fears and then find relief
7 One who can learn from one's feelings and experiences
9 The primary issue in bullying
11 The behaviors of someone who trusts and values himself or herself
12 A feeling we may not want others to know we have
15 How one's popularity may be viewed by another
17 What one may wish to do when rejected or excluded
18 The sacred promise within each and every person
19 What we all fear becoming
20 What someone does to us to cut us out or keep us separate
22 A disrespectful behavior that discounts another person

PUZZLE 12

PUZZLE 13

Across

1 The challenge by others to do something to prove one's courage
5 What traumatized youngsters often do
7 The internal sensing of high anxiety and danger
8 What false friends do
9 To take back one's personal power, internal strengths, and self-respect
12 Having no close connections or bonds with family
15 A sudden survival reaction to a perceived threat or danger
16 A type of security required by stressed, anxious youngsters
17 Focusing on an imaginary safe place while breathing deeply
19 The process of resolving the helplessness of trauma through drawing and journaling
21 The ability to put oneself in another's shoes; an ability that can be canceled out by trauma
23 Can be a survival reaction to feeling unsafe
26 Becomes a focus for youth who feel helpless after a trauma

Down

2 The behavioral pattern caused by trauma that is misunderstood and mislabeled
3 Someone who will support and stand up for a youngster
4 A condition that is essential for recovery from trauma to take place
6 An outline for assuring safety that is essential for certain locations
8 The false behaviors of someone who wants others to consider him or her to have a strong sense of self-worth
10 A type of message quickly detected by traumatized youth
11 The ability to control one's _____ can be put in jeopardy by trauma
12 Events caused by nature that can cause trauma
13 To talk about scary experiences, leading to relief
14 A kind of abuse that can cause deep, lasting hurts
18 A sudden, overwhelming experience of fright that causes feelings of helplessness
20 A condition resulting from a survival reaction that causes one to freeze or not be aware of feelings
22 As for not encountering a bully
24 A type of unsafe behavior traumatized youth engage in that can make them vulnerable
25 A bullying behavior intended to snub

PUZZLE 13

PUZZLE 14

Across

5 Official guidelines, which often fail to deal with bullying, especially by girls
7 What all mistreated youngsters want to hear from the instigators
8 The suggestion often given by adults to youngsters who complain about bullying
10 Abbreviation for United States
11 Abbreviation for recreation
12 Exclusive clan or group that behaves in a clannish way
13 Abbreviation for Underwriters Laboratory
14 Abbreviation for veteran
16 The conditions in which bullying is done
17 The kind of treatment imposed on girls targeted by girl bullies
18 Abbreviation for morning
21 The silent observer of bullying who has the power to end the maltreatment
23 What bullied students dread to hear as they prepare to move into the halls
24 A piercing stare
27 Pieces of information passed between students, sometimes with misinformation
29 To acquire
31 Abbreviation for "light" weight or low calories
32 Disgusting, mean, and spiteful
33 The arbitrary standards set by the leader of the bullies
35 Behavior by someone sad, lonely
36 Sarcastic name for girl bully
37 Slang for smelly
39 Affirmative, agreeable response
40 To extract information, to process clues
41 For some students, the end result of being harassed
42 What some teachers have in their classrooms

Down

1 Concealed, secret, hidden action
2 Intense fear creating an inability to think rationally
3 The bite of sarcastic words
4 What needs to be said to those who harass
6 A demeaning verbal assault
7 The way girls hurt other girls
9 Undisclosed cause of much of the bullying and harassing; seen as a threat by instigator
14 One form of abuse
15 Type of information spread by girl bullies, often untrue
19 To put into practice
20 Having ability, skills
22 The feeling of the one targeted by a bully as adults look the other way
23 A dare
25 To place down
26 Half the beginning of life for birds, reptiles, and mammals
28 To kill
30 Type of treatment that causes harm, pain, and sorrow
34 The results of rumors and harassment on the self-worth and the emotional state of mind of the target
36 Silence; what is normally heard from adults in response to bullying
38 The facial expressions of instigators when confronted
41 To weaken, undermine
43 Seventh tone in the scale

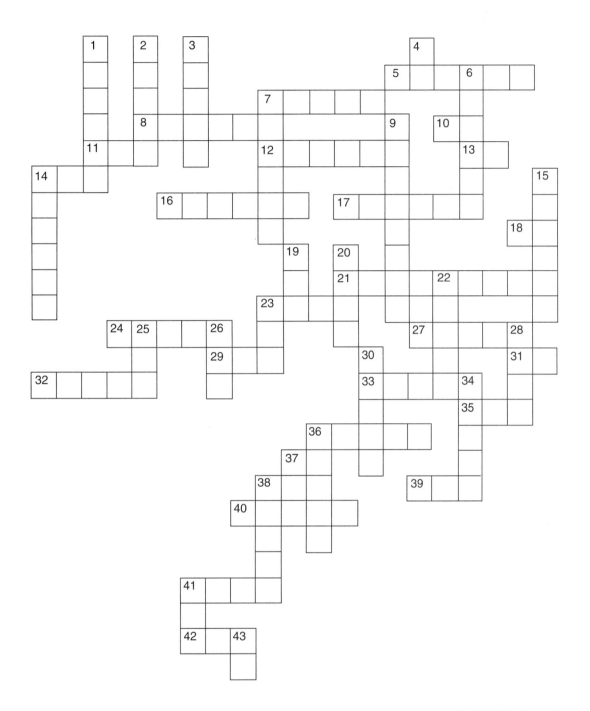

PUZZLE 14

PUZZLE 15

Across

5 The necessary process of building strong connections between parent and child

8 What someone cannot do by trying to talk youth out of traumatic behavior

9 Full recovery often results in finding new ones

12 What traumatized youngsters find hard to do for themselves

14 What trauma causes

18 Certain ones can trigger frightening memories

19 A property of the arts useful for recovering and becoming a survivor

20 To look at experiences of survival differently

24 A way of acting that can cover up toxic memories

25 Thoughts of terror that pop into one's mind and cause stress and fear

26 Someone who becomes the target of the anger over unresolved fears and losses

27 What becomes hard to do when traumatized

28 What traumatized youngsters yearn for

Down

1 What healed youngsters can once again do about their destiny or future

2 What needs to be restored for traumatized youth

3 The nightmares that trauma causes and that disrupt sleep

4 A kind of secret memory that can destroy self-worth

6 A feeling caused by toxic memories

7 What some traumatized youth try to become in order to feel better

10 What youngsters who do not have strong bonds join for belonging

11 Becomes the primary focus of traumatized youngsters

13 An essential activity for coping with what was lost or never provided

15 A certain kind of verbal abuse that can trigger toxic memories

16 What we often do to memories of fears and loss

17 To honor one's survival skills and sense of future

21 Troubling action that youngsters with toxic memories take to try not to remember

22 Where traumatic memories are lodged and why movement is necessary for healing

23 A new experience that triggers old memories of loss or fear

PUZZLE 15

PUZZLE 16

Across

1 What is spread by those who hope to be included and accepted by a certain group
5 Youngsters who can also be devastated by bullying and aggression
6 Something girls are not expected to do
10 People who give acceptance and glory to bullying
12 What adults seem unprepared to do about bullying
13 A form of girl bullying
15 The kind of effort required by a school to end bullying
16 Actions used to deliberately cause fears of exclusion
17 Used by someone to intimidate and humiliate
21 One way to reduce being bullied and build confidence
24 The kind of treatment given out by cliques
25 Groups held together by excluding others
26 What most youth who bully have been sometime or somewhere
28 Something even friends can be
29 A behavior that can be difficult to measure as true or false

Down

2 The feeling many bullies are afraid of feeling
3 What cliques try to do to others in order to feel more powerful
4 A verbal action that is intended to impose ridicule and helplessness on others
7 Spread by cliques to shame others
8 A common way for someone to end up that results from behavior by members of a clique
9 The requirement put on youth in order to be accepted and included
10 The behaviors sometimes engaged in by popular youth
11 The feeling that is the goal of those who impose humiliation
14 A creative way to respond to teasing and taunting
18 A student who cannot end bullying without the support of adults and peers
19 Used by cliques and bullies to enforce power, control, and fear
20 The type of choices a targeted youngster has a hard time seeing
22 How youngsters who bully are afraid of ending up
23 Sometimes part of rumors and silent treatments
27 A setup designed to intimidate or humiliate

PUZZLE 16

Resource B:
Answers to the
Crossword Puzzles

These crossword puzzle answers may be photocopied for student use.

ANSWERS FOR PUZZLE 1

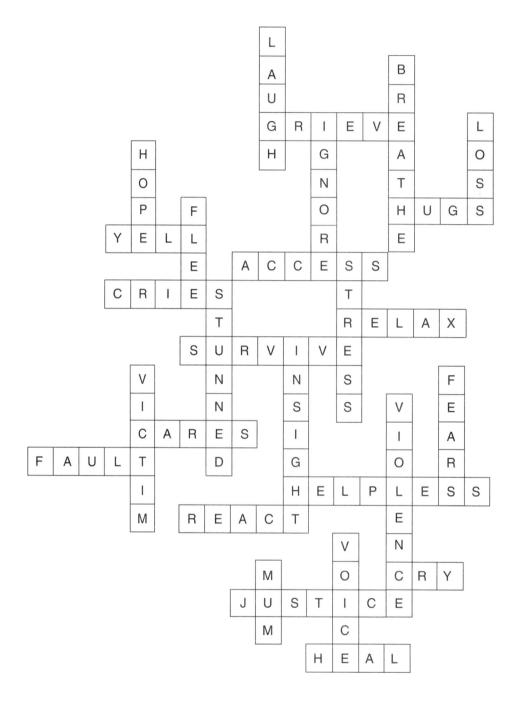

ANSWERS FOR PUZZLE 2

ANSWERS FOR PUZZLE 3

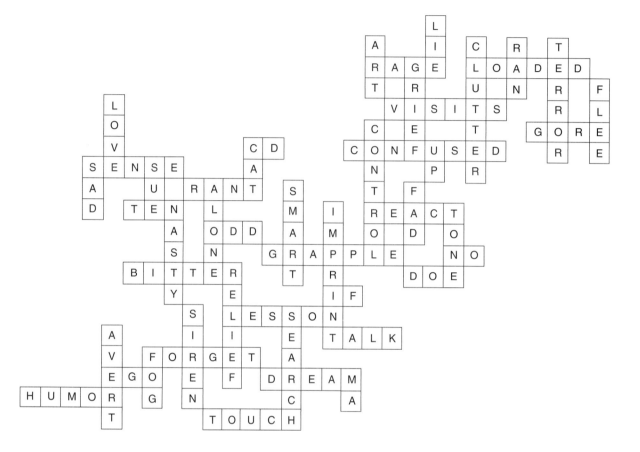

ANSWERS FOR PUZZLE 4

ANSWERS FOR PUZZLE 5

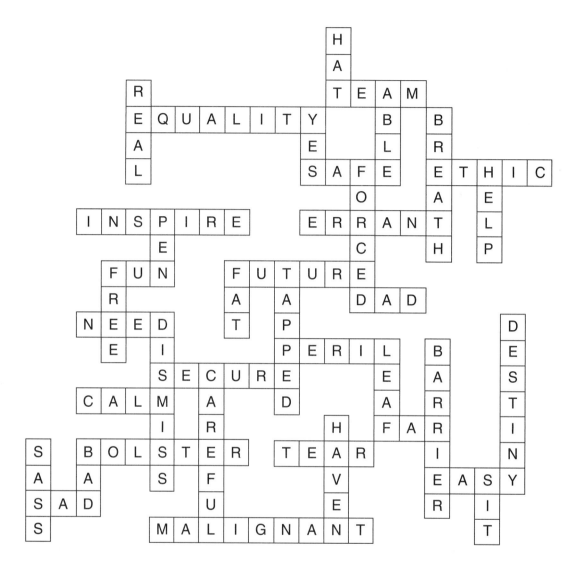

ANSWERS FOR PUZZLE 6

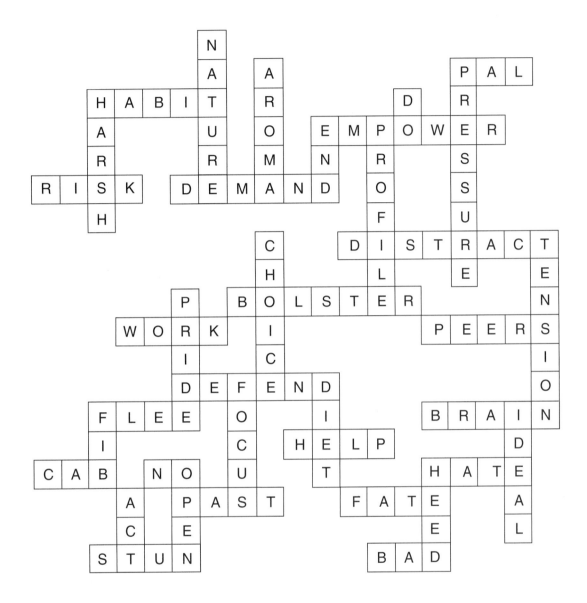

ANSWERS FOR PUZZLE 7

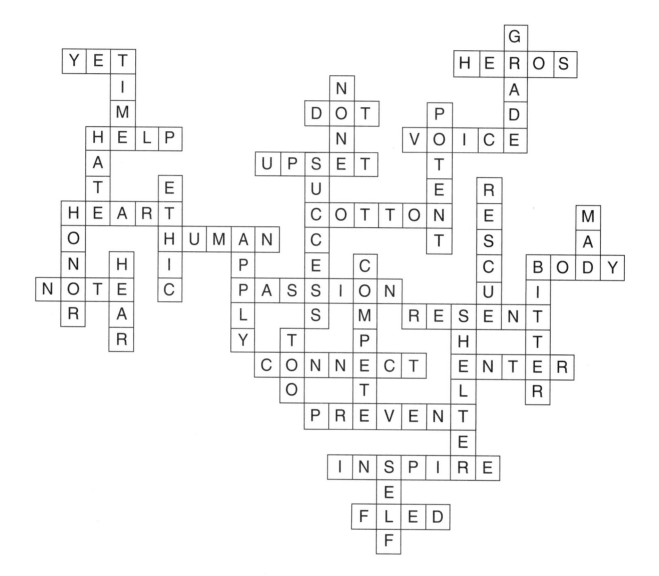

ANSWERS FOR PUZZLE 8

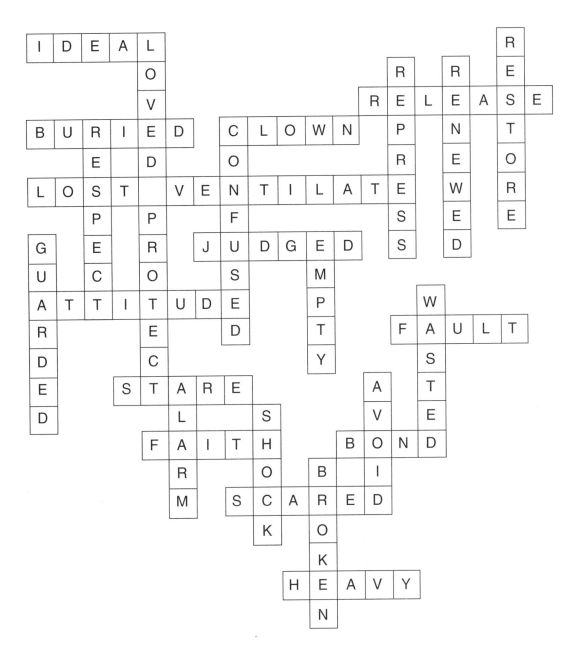

ANSWERS FOR PUZZLE 9

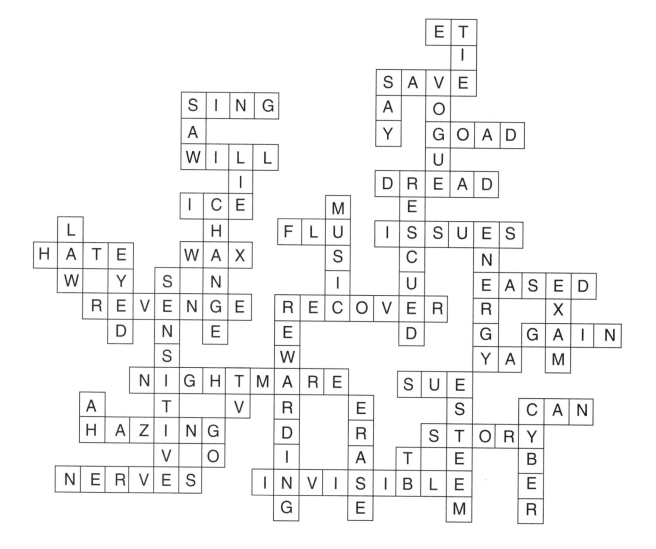

ANSWERS FOR PUZZLE 10

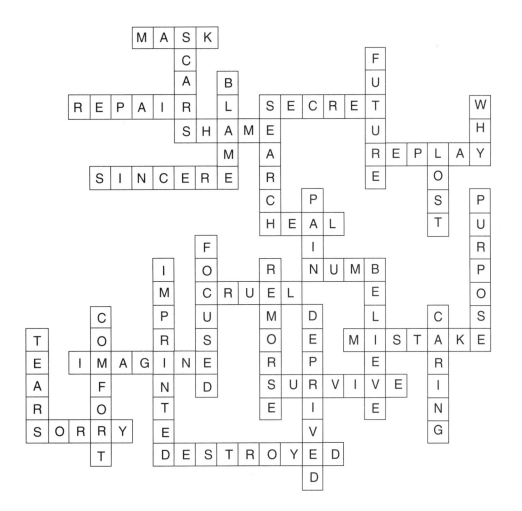

ANSWERS FOR PUZZLE 11

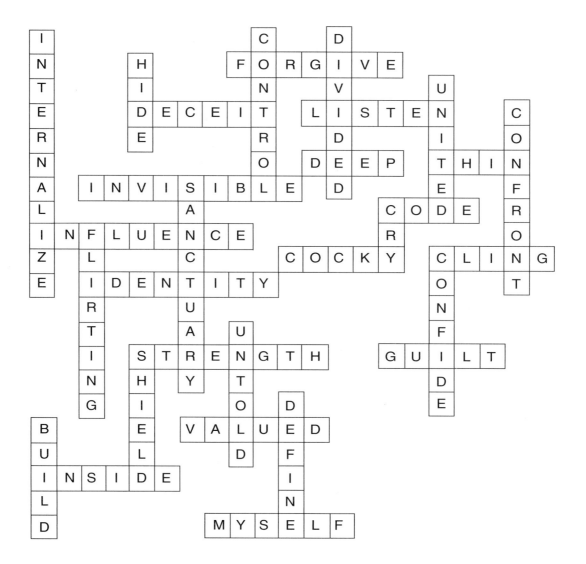

ANSWERS FOR PUZZLE 12

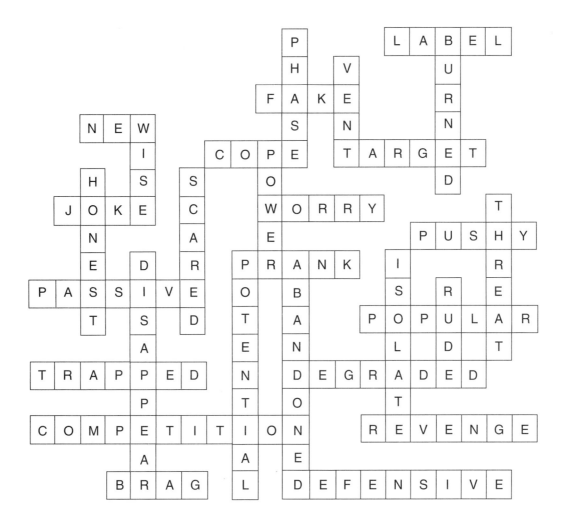

ANSWERS FOR PUZZLE 13

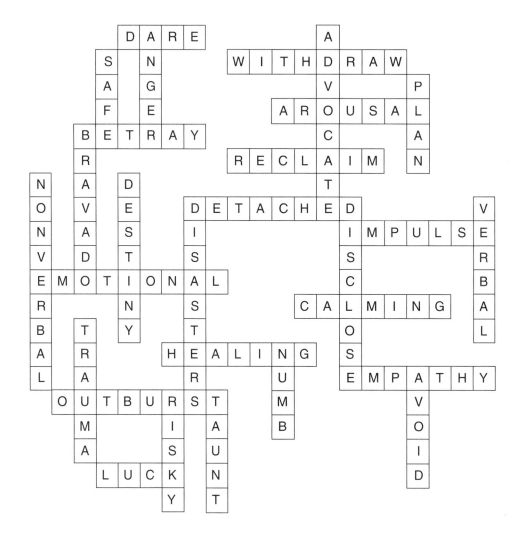

ANSWERS FOR PUZZLE 14

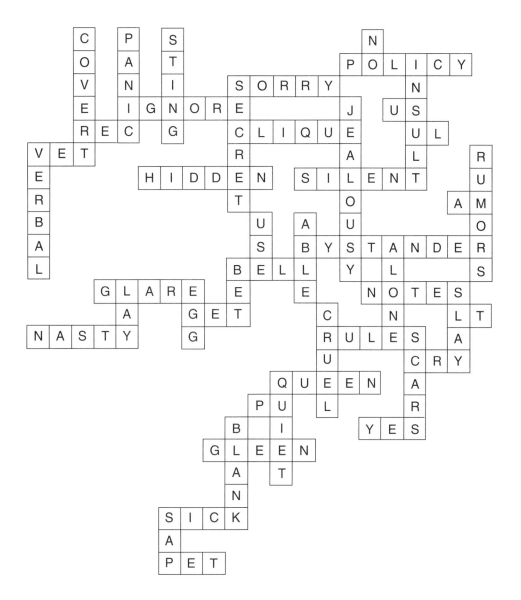

ANSWERS FOR PUZZLE 15

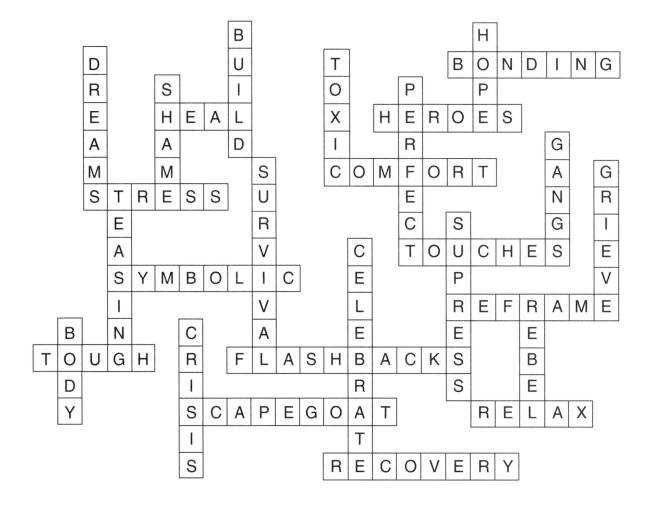

ANSWERS FOR PUZZLE 16

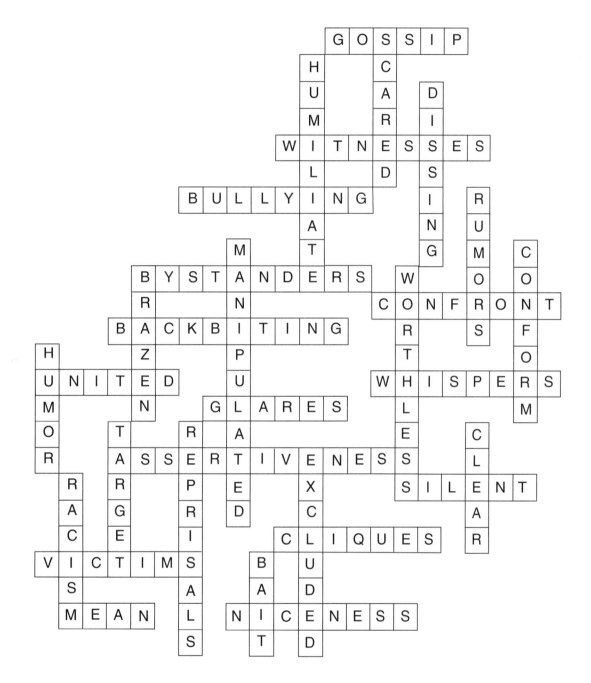

References

Allen, J. G. (2001). *Traumatic relationships and serious mental disorders.* Indianapolis, IN: John Wiley & Sons.

Allen, J. S., & Klein, R. (1996). *Ready, set, relax.* Watertown, WI: Inner Coaching.

Ayers, R. (2001). *Studs Terkel's working: A teaching guide.* New York: New Press.

Bailey, B. (2000). *I love you rituals.* New York: HarperCollins.

Bean, A. L. (1999). *Bully free classrooms.* Minneapolis, MN: Free Spirit Publishing.

Biagi, S. (1986). *Interviews that work.* Belmont, CA: Wadsworth.

Bloom, S. L., & Reichert, M. (1998). *Bearing witness: Violence and collective responsibility.* New York: Haworth.

Bovard, K. (2000). The Emotion Map. *Teaching Tolerance, 17,* 18–21.

Breggin, P. R. (2000). *Reclaiming our children: A healing plan for a nation in crisis.* Cambridge, MA: Perseus.

Bremner, J. D. (2002). *Does stress damage the brain?* New York: W. W. Norton.

Brohl, K., & Diaz, P. (1995). *Working with traumatized children: A handbook for healing.* Washington, DC: Child Welfare League of America.

Capacchione, L. (1989). *The creative journal for children: A guide for parents, teachers, and counselors.* Boston: Shambhala.

Claassen, R. (2000). Holistic discipline. *MCS Conciliation Quarterly, spring,* 2–3.

Corder, C., & Brohl, K. (1996). *It couldn't happen here: Recognizing and helping desperate kids.* Washington, DC: Child Welfare League of America.

Elias, M. J., & Zins, J. E. (2003). *Bullying, peer harassment and victimization in schools.* New York: Haworth.

Fincher, S. F. (1991). *Creating mandalas.* Boston: Shambhala.

Fogarty, J. A. (2000). *The magical thoughts of grieving children.* Amityville, NY: Bagwood.

Garbarino, J. (1995). *Raising children in a socially toxic environment.* San Francisco: Jossey-Bass.

Garbarino, J. (1999). *Lost boys: Why our sons turn violent and how we can save them.* New York: Free Press.

Garbarino, J., & deLara, E. (2002). *And words can hurt forever: How to protect adolescents from bullying, harassment, and emotional violence.* New York: Free Press.

Goldberg, C. M. (1999). *Write where you are.* Minneapolis, MN: Free Spirit Press.

Graham, J. (1999). *It's up to us: The giraffe heroes program.* Langley, WA: The Giraffe Project.

Greenwald, R. (2002). *Trauma and juvenile delinquency: Theory, research, and interventions.* New York: Haworth.

Henderson, N., & Benard, M. M. (1996). *Resiliency in schools: Making it happen for students and educators.* Thousand Oaks, CA: Corwin.

Hyman, I., & Snook, P. (1999). *Dangerous schools: What we can do about the physical and emotional abuse of our children.* San Francisco, CA: Jossey-Bass.

Kagan, R. (2004). *Rebuilding attachments with traumatized children: Healing from losses, violence, abuse, and neglect.* New York: Haworth.

Karr-Morse, R., & Wiley, M. S. (1997). *Ghosts from the nursery: Tracing the roots of violence.* New York: Atlantic Monthly Press.

Kielburger, C. (1998). *Free the children.* Toronto, Ontario: McClelland & Stewart.

Meier, D., Kohn, A., Darling-Hammond, L., Sizer, T. R., & Wood, G. (2004). *Many children left behind.* Boston: Beacon.

Niehoff, D. (1999). *The biology of violence.* New York: Free Press.

Oehlberg, B. (1996). *Making it better: Activities for children living in a stressful world.* St. Paul, MN: Redleaf.

Perry, B. D. (Producer). (2002). Identifying and responding to trauma in ages six to adolescence (video five of six) [videotape]. (Available from Magna Systems, http://www.magna systems.org)

Pollack, W. (1998). *Real boys: Rescuing our sons from the myth of boyhood.* New York: Henry Holt.

Rothschild, B. (2000). *The body remembers: The psychophysiology of trauma and trauma treatment.* New York: W. W. Norton.

Saltzman, W. R., Pynoos, R. S., Layne, C. M., Steinberg, A. M., & Aisenberg, E. (2001). Trauma and grief-focused interventions for adolescents exposed to community violence: Results of a school-based screening and group treatment protocol. *Theory, Research, Practice, 5*(4), 291–303.

Silva, R. R. (2004). *Post-traumatic stress disorders in children & adolescents.* New York: W. W. Norton.

Solomon, M. F., & Siegel, D. (2003). *Healing trauma: Attachment, mind, body & brain.* New York: W. W. Norton.

Steele, W. (1998). *Trauma debriefing for schools and agencies.* Grosse Pointe Woods, MI: TLC Institute.

Steele, W. (1999). *Kids on the inside: Looking out after loss.* Grosse Pointe Woods, MI: TLC Institute.

Stuecker, R., & Rutherford, S. (2001). *Reviving the wonder: 76 activities that touch the inner spirit of youth.* Champaign, IL: Research Press.

Terr, L. (1990). *Too scared to cry.* New York: Basic Books.

Walker, A. From a presentation at the National Institute of Trauma and Loss in Children, Grosse Pointe Woods, MI.

Index

Abuse/neglect, 13, 19, 52–53
Academic achievement, 21, 55–56, 77–81,
    86–88, 94, 103
Adrenal system, 49
Afterschool programs
    board game design, 59–60
    clubs, 64–67, 73
    crossword puzzles, 67, 107–157
    logo design, 56–57
    physical/mental exercises, 60
    plays, puppets, and masks, 57–59
    safety/security activity, 60–62
    sand trays, 63–64
    value of, 55–56, 66, 73
Aggression
    as self-preservation, 96
    brain activity and, 20
    causes of, 91–92
    cognitive lockout and, 15
    impulsive, 87, 94
    in males, 13
    reducing, 78, 94
    research on, 43
    See also Behavior
Allen, Jeffrey, 54
Amygdala, 14, 15, 18, 19
Anger. *See* Behavior, angry
Anxiety. *See* Stress
Arts, benefits of, 18, 31–32, 48–49, 67. *See also*
    Language arts; Theater/arts groups
Attachment, 13, 14, 15, 43, 45
Attention deficit/hyperactivity
    disorder, 15
Autonomic nervous system, 19

Bailey, Becky, 20, 81
Behavior
    aggressive. *See* Aggression
    angry, 13, 78, 80, 91, 93–94
    causes of problem, 79
    changes in, 15, 52, 92

changing, 15, 19–21, 43. *See also*
    Interventions
    choice and, 43
    clues to, 20
    compliant, 52
    inappropriate, 43, 77–81, 91
    responding to, 78–83
    triggers, 15
    victims of mis-, 80
Bipolar disorder, 15
Bovard, Karen, 45
Boy Scouts, 73
Boys and Girls Clubs, 73
Brain development, 13–14
Brain, areas of, 14 (figure)
Buddy programs, 89–90
Bullying. *See* School safety, bullying

Central nervous system, 18, 43, 52
Character education
    activities for, 44–52
    board game, 51–52
    box of respect, 47
    character wall, 50–51
    classroom directory of feelings/
        emotions, 44–45
    coaching, 44
    defined, 44
    drawing a dream, 48–49
    facing fears, 49
    feelings mural, 45–46
    heroes and, 50–52
    iceberg project, 47–48
    importance of, 43–44
    letters to hurts, 48
    playground charters, 49–50
    resources for, 54
Child abuse, 19
Classroom change
    alternative responses and, 78–79
    avoiding threats and, 78

guidelines for, 79–83
rules, 79–80
stress reduction and, 81–83
transition times and, 81–82
Clubs, 64–67, 73, 100
Cognitive lockout
and memory, 15, 78
defined, 14
effects of, 14–17, 78
learning and, 15, 17, 78
personal safety and, 15
See also Brain development; Memory
Community support, 86–88, 91–92, 95, 104–105
Conduct disorder, 15
Conflict and anger management.
See School safety, conflict and
anger management
Conflict Resolution in American
History, 94
Cortex, 78
Cortisol, 16, 52
Council of Chief State School Officers, 85, 86
Creating Mandalas, 34
Creative writing
ad campaigns, 32
betrayal and, 26, 28
comic books, 32–33
confidentiality and, 26
debating points and, 30
drawing combined with, 31–33
emotional intelligence and, 26, 28–29
empowerment and, 26, 29–30
examples of, 26–34, 48, 49, 67–68, 71
helplessness and, 26, 27–28
importance of, 25–26, 31
loss/rejection and, 26–27
prose and poetry, 30–31
Crisis preparation. *See* school safety,
crisis preparation
Crossword puzzles, 67, 107–157

Dance, 68–70
DeLara, E., 95, 96
Discipline
defined, 80
for bullying, 95–96
goals of, 80, 101
policies, 94–95
prevention and, 94–102
punitive, 80, 87, 92, 101
resources for, 101–102
restorative, 80–81, 91–92, 100–102
suspension/expulsion as, 91–92

Discipline That Restores (DTR), 80–81
Dogs, therapy, 82
Domestic violence, 13
Drawing, 18, 25–26, 31–32, 48–49.
See also Arts, benefits of
Drop-outs, 88, 99, 100
Drug use, 100

Education
change in, 103–104
cooperative, 103
leadership in, 85–88
politicization of, 86
reform, 85, 103
Einstein, Albert, 51
Emotional
development, 86
intelligence, 26, 28–29, 44
needs, 86
Empathy, fostering, 66, 90
Empowerment, 18, 73, 87, 95–96
Exclusion/rejection, 26–27, 96, 99–100

Fear, 49, 52, 78, 95–96
Fight/flight/freeze reaction, 13, 78, 87
Fincher, Susanne F., 34
Fire drill *versus* safety drill, 93
Flashbacks, 15
Fogarty, James, 11
Four-H Clubs, 73
Free the Children USA, 65
Futurelessness, 87–88

Gangs, 73, 100
Garbarino, J., 95, 96
Girl Scouts, 73
Glossary, 5–7
Goldberg, Caryn Mirriam, 26
Good Grief Program, The, 82
Graham, John, 49
Greenwald, Ricky, 43
Grief, 82, 92

Healing Arts Project, 83
Helplessness
and language arts. *See* Language arts
character education and. *See* Character
education
parental, 87
transforming, 17–20, 49–50, 52, 79, 81, 94
Heroes, 50–52
Hippocampus, 16, 52
History projects

artistic media, 38–41
    cartoons and storyboards, 36–37
    fictional comic books, 37
    importance of, 35
    public service announcements, 40–41
    radio scripts, 38–40
    symbolic projection and, 35
    topics for, 36–41
Homeostasis, 19
Hyman, Irwin A., 91
Hyperactivity, 15, 52
Hypersensitivity, 15, 21, 81
Hypervigilance, 15, 21, 45

I Feel Better Now, 82
Imaging, 53
Immigrant students, 90
Incest, 52–53
Inclusion, 99–100
Individual educational plan, 89
Inner Coaching, 53
Internal strengths, 44, 51
Interventions
    early, 80, 94–95
    frequency of, 19
    importance of, 18–19
    language arts. *See* Creative writing;
        Language arts
    research on, 18
    resources for, 18–19
    school-based, 18
    transformative, 43–44, 56
    trauma-specific, 91–92
    versus prevention, 94
    See also Afterschool programs; Clubs;
        Theater/arts groups
It's Up to Us: The Giraffe Heroes
        Program, 49

Journaling, 18, 25–26, 48. *See also*
    Creative writing

Kagan, R., 96
Keller, Helen, 44
Kielburger, Craig, 65
Klein, Roger, 54
Kocs, Katherine J., 95

Language arts
    creative writing. *See* Creative writing
    flexibility and, 25
    grammar/spelling and, 25
    importance of, 25–26, 31

symbolic, 25
    See also Creative writing; Journaling
Leadership, 49–50, 73, 85–88
Learning
    by anxious students, 85–86
    cortical, 78
    process of, 85
    See also Academic achievement;
        Memory
Life interviews, 91
Limbic systems, 13, 14, 20, 49
Losses
    anger and, 12
    behaviors resulting from, 12, 43. *See also*
        Behavior
    concrete operations and, 11–12
    effects of, 11–12, 89
    family and, 11
    types of, 12
    unresolved, 12
    See also Creative writing, loss/rejection and

Magical Thoughts of Grieving Children,
        The, 11
Making It Better, 79
Males, aggression in, 13. *See also* Aggression
Mandalas, 33–34
Media role, 104
Mediation, 101
Memory
    cognitive lockout and, 15, 78
    hippocampus and, 16
    internal, 18
    storage of, 15, 18
    See also Learning
Mentoring, 89
Midbrain systems, 13
Middle schools, 89
Mind-body integration, 19–20, 52. *See also*
        Self–regulation
Muscle relaxation, 53–54
Music, 53, 68–70

National Assessment of Educational
        Progress, 77
National Longitudinal Study of Adolescent
        Health, 77
Neocortex, 14, 15, 18, 19, 20, 25
Neural integration, 19
Neurobiology
    alterations, 18, 45
    and educational strategies, 85
    interpersonal, 19

research on, 13–14, 85–86, 103
  See also Cognitive lockout
New/transferring students, 90
No Child Left Behind, 14, 85
Nonverbal expressions, interpreting, 45

One Million Postcards, 65

Parental input, 16, 56, 87, 88, 95, 101, 104
Perry, Bruce D., 13
Physical activities, 66
Physical strengths, 52–54
Police officers, 87
Pollack, William, 90
Posttraumatic stress disorder, 13
Pre-frontal cortex, 13, 14, 19, 20
Preadolescent rage, 13. *See also* Aggression;
  Behavior, angry
Professional development, 86
PRYME, 71
Psychomotor activity, 18, 66
Pynoos, Robert, 18

Ready, Set, Relax, 54
Reentering students, 89–90
Rejection, 90, 96
Relationships, importance of, 80–81, 86, 89
Relaxation techniques, 52–54
Resiliency
  activities for building, 55–67
  importance of, 55
  restoring academic, 78–80
Restorative justice. *See* Discipline, restorative
Retraumatization, 25

Safe Harbor Project, The, 83
Safety/security
  activities for fostering, 60–62, 73
  brain function and, 20
  emotional, 20, 81, 86
  environmental, 44
  fostering feelings of, 20, 52
  personal, 15
  school. *See* School safety
Saltzman, William, 18
School nurses, 94
School safety
  armed officers and, 87
  bullying, 95–99
  conflict and anger management,
    93–94, 96
  crisis preparation, 92–93
  empowering students and, 87, 95–96

game, 96–98
holistic *versus* structural, 88
importance of, 78–80, 85–88, 91, 95
middle school, 89
resources for, 99
school culture and, 95
strategies for promoting, 87–90, 96
suspension/expulsion policies and,
  91–92
violence and, 91–102. *See also* Violence
weapons and, 87, 91, 100
zero tolerance. *See* Zero tolerance
School size, 89
School-Based Mourning Project, 83
Self-regulation, 13, 14, 19–21, 20
Sensory activities, 18
Sensory triggers, 15
Sexual abuse, 52–53
Social action, 65–66
Social studies. *See* History projects
Standards for School Leaders, 86
Steele, William, 93
Sticks and Stones, 95
Stress
  brain development and, 13
  destructive behavior and, 13
  effects of, 13, 78
  hormones, 16
  management, 52–54, 56, 79–83, 87
  symptoms of, 81
  teaching styles and, 17, 81, 86
  traumatic, 13, 15. *See also* Trauma;
    Traumatic memories
Suicide, 95
Summer camps, 71–73
Suspension and expulsion policies, 91–92

Teachers
  changing styles of, 17, 86, 103–104
  classroom environment and, 81–83.
    See also Classroom change
  relationships with students, 77
  support for, 104
  transition times for, 81
Terrorist attacks, 15, 50, 91, 92
Test taking, 15, 78
Theater/arts groups
  comedy script writing, 68
  drama script writing, 67–68
  media production, 71
  movement and dance, 68–69
  resources for, 69, 71
  rhythm, 69–70

value of, 67. 73
See also Arts, benefits of
Therapy Dogs International, 82
Threats
   defining, 92
   perception of, 94
   removing, 87
   responding to, 78–79, 94
   suspension/expulsion, 91–92
TLC Institute, 92
Trauma
   -specific interventions, 91–92, 94
   effects of, 88
   examples of, 15, 89–90
   singular *versus* secondhand, 15
   training in, 94–95
   See also Stress; Traumatic memories
Trauma and Juvenile Delinquency, 43
Trauma Debriefing for Schools and
     Agencies, 93
Traumatic memories
   erasing/defusing, 18, 43
   externalization of, 18, 43
   managing, 18, 21, 52, 56. *See also*
      Interventions; Self–regulation

triggering, 13–15
   See also Loss; Trauma
Trust, restoring, 80, 87

Victims, 95–98
Violence
   as a survival mechanism, 13, 94
   bullying. *See* School safety, bullying
   family, 96
   prevention, 94–102
   restorative justice and, 100–101
   weapons and, 87, 91, 100
   zero tolerance and, 91. *See also* Zero
     tolerance
   See also School safety

Walker, Anita, 92
Why Students Need to Feel Safe in School,
    96–98
Write Where You Are, 26

Young African American Women teen
    program, 73

Zero tolerance, 26, 35, 91–92

**CORWIN
PRESS**

The Corwin Press logo—a raven striding across an open book—represents the union of courage and learning. Corwin Press is committed to improving education for all learners by publishing books and other professional development resources for those serving the field of PreK–12 education. By providing practical, hands-on materials, Corwin Press continues to carry out the promise of its motto: **"Helping Educators Do Their Work Better."**